S.O.S. FOR WINDOWS™

by Katherine Murray

IDG Books

San Mateo, California

S.O.S. For Windows

Published by
IDG Books Worldwide, Inc.
An International Data Group Company
155 Bovet Road, Suite 310
San Mateo, CA 94402

Text and art copyright © 1993 by IDG Books Worldwide. All rights reserved. No part of this book may be reproduced or transmitted in any form, by any means (electronic, photocopying, recording, or otherwise) without the prior written permission of the publisher.

Library of Congress Catalog Card No.: 93-080352

ISBN: 1-56884-045-4

Printed in the United States of America

10 9 8 7 6 5 4 3 2 1

Distributed in the United States by IDG Books Worldwide, Inc.

Distributed in Canada by Macmillan of Canada, a Division of Canada Publishing Corporation; by Computer and Technical Books in Miami, Florida, for South America and the Caribbean; by Longman Singapore in Singapore, Malaysia, Thailand, and Korea; by Toppan Co. Ltd. in Japan, by Asia Computerworld in Hong Kong; by Woodslane Pty. Ltd. in Australia and New Zealand; and by Transworld Publishers Ltd. in the U.K. and Europe.

For information on where to purchase IDG Books outside the U.S., contact Christina Turner at 415-312-0633. For information on translations, contact Marc Jeffrey Mikulich, Foreign Rights Manager, at IDG Books Worldwide; FAX NUMBER 415-358-1260.

For sales inquiries and special prices for bulk quantities, write to the address above or call IDG Books Worldwide at 415-312-0650.

Limit of Liability/Disclaimer of Warranty: The author and publisher have used their best efforts in preparing this book. IDG Books Worldwide, Inc., International Data Group, Inc., and the author makes no representation or warranties with respect to the accuracy or completeness of the contents of this book and specifically disclaim any implied warranties or merchantability or fitness for any particular purpose and shall in no event be liable for any loss of profit or any other commercial damage, including but not limited to special, incidental, consequential, or other damages.

Trademarks: All brand names and product names used in this book are trademarks, registered trademarks, or trade names of their respective holders. IDG Books Worldwide is not associated with any product or vendor mentioned in this book.

Dedication

To Doug, who makes everything possible

Acknowledgments

Forging a series as unique and creative as this one is an (almost) indescribably difficult process. Thanks to the insight, input, and inspiration of the following people:

David Solomon, Publisher, for his initial vision and continuing input,

Laurie Smith, Project Editor, for her keen understanding of this series and her vision of the end product; and for shepherding the myriad of pieces, all in the right directions, and all in an impossible amount of time,

Christopher Rozzi, Illustrator, for his amazing ability to bring characters to life before our eyes,

John Kaufeld, Technical Editor, for the many terrific suggestions and comments that helped put and keep the book on target,

My agent, Claudette Moore, for continuing her role as the director of PCSEO (Provider of Constructive Suggestions for the Emotionally Overwrought),

Beth Jenkins and Bill Hartman, for their unrelenting pursuit of the ultimate design, and Cindy Phipps, Valery Bourke, Gina Scott, and the rest of the Production department, for all of their hard work and patience,

Julie King, Tim Gallan, Barbara Potter, Sharon Hilgenberg, and Chuck Hutchinson for their unfailing and unflagging attention to detail,

My family — Doug, Kelly, Christopher, and Cameron — for their Extra Effort, which made my Extra Effort possible.

Katherine Murray

(The publisher would like to give special thanks to Patrick J. McGovern, without whom this book would not have been possible.)

About IDG Books Worldwide

Welcome to the world of IDG Books Worldwide.

IDG Books Worldwide, Inc., is a division of International Data Group, the world's largest publisher of computer-related information and the leading global provider of information services on information technology. IDG publishes over 194 computer publications in 62 countries. Forty million people read one or more IDG publications each month.

If you use personal computers, IDG Books is committed to publishing quality books that meet your needs. We rely on our extensive network of publications, including such leading periodicals as *Macworld*, *InfoWorld*, *PC World*, *Computerworld*, *Publish*, *Network World*, and *SunWorld*, to help us make informed and timely decisions in creating useful computer books that meet your needs.

Every IDG book strives to bring extra value and skill-building instruction to the reader. Our books are written by experts, with the backing of IDG periodicals, and with careful thought devoted to issues such as audience, interior design, use of icons, and illustrations. Our editorial staff is a careful mix of high-tech journalists and experienced book people. Our close contact with the makers of computer products helps ensure accuracy and thorough coverage. Our heavy use of personal computers at every step in production means we can deliver books in the most timely manner.

We are delivering books of high quality at competitive prices on topics customers want. At IDG, we believe in quality, and we have been delivering quality for over 25 years. You'll find no better book on a subject than an IDG book.

    John Kilcullen
    President and C.E.O.
    IDG Books Worldwide, Inc.

IDG Books Worldwide, Inc. is a division of International Data Group. The officers are Patrick J. McGovern, Founder and Board Chairman; Walter Boyd, President. International Data Group's publications include: ARGENTINA's Computerworld Argentina, InfoWorld Argentina; ASIA's Computerworld Hong Kong, PC World Hong Kong, Computerworld Southeast Asia, PC World Singapore, Computerworld Malaysia, PC World Malaysia; AUSTRALIA's Computerworld Australia, Australian PC World, Australian Macworld, Network World, Reseller, IDG Sources; AUSTRIA's Computerwelt Oesterreich, PC Test; BRAZIL's Computerworld, Mundo IBM, Mundo Unix, PC World, Publish; BULGARIA's Computerworld Bulgaria, Ediworld, PC & Mac World Bulgaria; CANADA's Direct Access, Graduate Computerworld, InfoCanada, Network World Canada; CHILE's Computerworld, Informatica; COLOMBIA's Computerworld Colombia; CZECH REPUBLIC's Computerworld, Elektronika, PC World; DENMARK's CAD/CAM WORLD, Communications World, Computerworld Danmark, LOTUS World, Macintosh Produktkatalog, Macworld Danmark, PC World Danmark, PC World Produktguide, Windows World; EQUADOR's PC World; EGYPT's Computerworld (CW) Middle East, PC World Middle East; FINLAND's MikroPC, Tietoviikko, Tietoverkko; FRANCE's Distributique, GOLDEN MAC, InfoPC, Languages & Systems, Le Guide du Monde Informatique, Le Monde Informatique, Telecoms & Reseaux; GERMANY's Computerwoche, Computerwoche Focus, Computerwoche Extra, Computerwoche Karriere, Information Management, Macwelt, Netzwelt, PC Welt, PC Woche, Publish, Unit; HUNGARY's Alaplap, Computerworld SZT, PC World, ; INDIA's Computers & Communications; ISRAEL's Computerworld Israel, PC World Israel; ITALY's Computerworld Italia, Lotus Magazine, Macworld Italia, Networking Italia, PC World Italia; JAPAN's Computerworld Japan, Macworld Japan, SunWorld Japan, Windows World; KENYA's East African Computer News; KOREA's Computerworld Korea, Macworld Korea, PC World Korea; MEXICO's Compu Edicion, Compu Manufactura, Computacion/Punto de Venta, Computerworld Mexico, MacWorld, Mundo Unix, PC World, Windows; THE NETHERLAND'S Computer! Totaal, LAN Magazine, MacWorld; NEW ZEALAND's Computer Listings, Computerworld New Zealand, New Zealand PC World; NIGERIA's PC World Africa; NORWAY's Computerworld Norge, C/World, Lotusworld Norge, Macworld Norge, Networld, PC World Ekspress, PC World Norge, PC World's Product Guide, Publish World, Student Data, Unix World, Windowsworld, IDG Direct Response; PANAMA's PC World; PERU's Computerworld Peru, PC World; PEOPLES REPUBLIC OF CHINA's China Computerworld, PC World China, Electronics International, China Network World; IDG HIGH TECH BEIJING's New Product World; IDG SHENZHEN's Computer News Digest; PHILLIPPINES' Computerworld, PC World; POLAND's Computerworld Poland, PC World/Komputer; PORTUGAL's Cerebro/PC World, Correio Informatico/Computerworld, MacIn; ROMANIA's PC World; RUSSIA's Computerworld-Moscow, Mir-PC, Sety; SLOVENIA's Monitor Magazine; SOUTH AFRICA's Computing S.A.; SPAIN's Amiga World, Computerworld Espana, Communicaciones World, Macworld Espana, NeXTWORLD, PC World Espana, Publish, Sunworld; SWEDEN's Attack, ComputerSweden, Corporate Computing, Lokala Natverk/LAN, Lotus World, MAC&PC, Macworld, Mikrodatorn, PC World, Publishing & Design (CAP), Datalngenjoren, Maxi Data, Windows World; SWITZERLAND's Computerworld Schweiz, Macworld Schweiz, PC & Workstation; TAIWAN's Computerworld Taiwan, Global Computer Express, PC World Taiwan; THAILAND's Thai Computerworld; TURKEY's Computerworld Monitor, Macworld Turkiye, PC World Turkiye; UNITED KINGDOM's Lotus Magazine, Macworld, Sunworld; UNITED STATES' AmigaWorld, Cable in the Classroom, CD Review, CIO, Computerworld, Desktop Video World, DOS Resource Guide, Electronic News, Federal Computer Week, Federal Integrator, GamePro, IDG Books, InfoWorld, InfoWorld Direct, Laser Event, Macworld, Multimedia World, Network World, NeXTWORLD, PC Games, PC Letter, PC World Publish, Sumeria, SunWorld, SWATPro, Video Event; VENEZUELA's Computerworld Venezuela, MicroComputerworld Venezuela; VIETNAM's PC World Vietnam

About the author

Long on the receiving end of computer problems, Katherine Murray has been a computer user since the early '80s, when, at home with an infant daughter and an 8088, she began a writing career that would eventually take her through 37 computer books, across platforms (PC and Mac), and into a world of computer trouble. She enjoys writing the S.O.S. series because it gives her a chance to commiserate with other computer users who, like her, often "Panic first and think later."

About the illustrator

Christopher Rozzi has illustrated several computer books in his free time, when he's not wearing his other hat as an indispensable exhibit artist at the Children's Museum in Indianapolis. He somehow managed to find the time to get married recently, which was amazing because we have kept him busy illustrating every hour of the day and night. Chris is an avid comic book collector, and he enjoys scuba diving, hiking, relaxing with his wife, Susan, and deciphering the various personalities of Lagniappe, their cat.

Credits

Publisher
David Solomon

Managing Editor
Mary Bednarek

Acquisitions Editor
Janna Custer

Production Manager
Beth Jenkins

Senior Editors
Sandy Blackthorn
Diane Graves Steele

Production Coordinator
Cindy L. Phipps

Acquisitions Assistant
Megg Bonar

Editorial Assistants
Patricia R. Reynolds
Darlene Cunningham

Project Editor
Laurie Ann Smith

Illustrator
Christopher Rozzi

Story Line
Christopher Rozzi
Laurie Ann Smith

Editors
Tim Gallan
Julie King
Barbara Potter

Technical Reviewer
John Kaufeld

Production Staff
Valery Bourke
Gina Scott

Proofreader
Charles A. Hutchinson

Indexer
Sharon Hilgenberg

Book Design
Beth Jenkins
William Hartman
Accent Technical
 Communications

Consultants
Brenda Dalton
Barry W. Eakle
Marti Icenogle
John Kaufeld
Brian J. Raby
Anna M. Shaw

Table of Contents

Prologue 3
Welcome to S.O.S. For Windows 4
Navigating through the Book 4
When You First Encounter Windows 6

Part I: What Happened? Where Am I? 9

1 Off to a Bad Start 13
Paths through Peril 13
My Computer Doesn't Work 14
WYSIN (What-You-See-Is-Nothing) 16
What Does Windows Want from Me? 17
Okay, Let's Go! 17
Pretty Hefty Program! 20

Crawling Installing	21
Sleuthing Screwy Setups	24
What Kind of Monitor Is That?	25
What Kind of Printer Is That?	25
Appalling Reinstalling	26
Windows No Like TSRs	27
Incompatible Differences	29
You Just Can't WIN	30
No-Go Windows	30
Headache A La Mode	32
Maybe I Will, Maybe I Won't	32
Time-Warp Windows	34
Here It Comes Again!	35
Where Is It?	36
The Case of the Dead Mouse	37
Mouse-Cicles	37
One Blind Mouse	38
Nuttin' Doin'	39
This Looks Awful!	39
Reading Smoke Signals	40
You Know You're Really in Trouble When...	42

2 Program Manager Perils 43

Paths through Peril	43
Program Manager Lite	45
Short, Fat Program Manager	46
Spots Before Your Eyes	46
Clashing Colors	47
Now Entering the Screen Saver Zone	47
Fool-Safe Screen Saving	48
Disappearing Program Groups	49
Go Nowhere Icons	50
Attack of the Weirdo Icons	51
Starting Nuthin'	51
Come On and Join the Group	52

Table of Contents

My Program Manager Doesn't Look Like That! 53
C'Mon, Now, Share! 54
Window Gigantus 55
Thin-Skinned Borders 55
Missing Window 58
It's All How You Look at It 59
Off the Wall(paper) Windows 59
But I Closed the Window! 61
Reading Smoke Signals 62
You Know You're Really in Trouble When. 64

3 File Manager Fiascoes 67
Paths through Peril 67
All I've Got Is a Tree 70
Unreadable File Manager 70
Directory Windows Everywhere 71
You Formatted What? 71
The Invisible Disk 72
File Manager's Not Listening 73
That's Not What's on My Disk! 73
All My Graphics Files Are Gone! 74
Disk Copy Flops 75
Sorry, No Association 76
Directory in Hiding 77
A File-Selection Nightmare 78
Let My Files Go! 79
Scrambled Files and Toast 80
Am I Moving or Copying? 81
Delete Terrors 84
Reading Smoke Signals 86
You Know You're Really in Trouble When. 87

4 Wicked Windows Applications 89
Paths through Peril 89
The Bad Install 90
The Big Lock Up 94

Finding Fault for Multiple Lockups 95
GPF Doesn't Mean Go Play Football 96
Afraid of Germs? 98
The Data Linking Game 99
Is OLE a Lot of Bull? 100
The DDE Connection 101
Multiple DDE Injuries 102
Where's DDE When You Need It? 103
Too Much Updating Going On 103
Reading Smoke Signals 104
You Know You're Really in Trouble When. 106

Part II: Where Do I Go Now? 108

5 Devilish DOS Programs 111
Paths through Peril 111
DOS Programs in Standard Mode 114
No Way Out 115
Forcing DOS Windows 115
The DOS Clipboard? 116
Moving Data from DOS to Windows 118
Squashed DOS Fonts 118
Two DOS Is Too Much 119
Short RAMs 120
From the Murky Depths: The Swap File 121
Where Do PIFs Come From? 121
Should You Modify Your PIFs? 122
Runs, but Not in the Right Place 124
Anyone Care for Fried Data? 125
Can't Get Screen Shots 126
No Deposit, No Return 127
No Paste-O? 127
Too Many Graphics 128
Strange Displays 128
My TSR Is SOL 130

Table of Contents

    Windowed Lockup 131
    Reading Smoke Signals 132
    You Know You're Really in Trouble When. 134

6 False Fonts 135
    Paths through Peril 135
    Disappearing Soft Fonts 136
    Me, Small Font! 137
    I Don't Have TrueType (Do I?) 137
    Foiled Font Installation 138
    The Case of the Missing Font Button 139
    Printer Blindness 139
    Godzilla Characters 141
    Fickle Fonts 141
    Psyched-Out in Font Land 144
    Can My Printer Print TrueType Fonts? 144
    TrueType Alone? 145
    GPFs in Font Land 146
    Font Lockup 148
    Changing Over Old Documents 148
    Slow Screen 150
    No Room for Fonts 153
    Monitor or Font Problems? 154
    Fonts Lost! 156
    PostScript Means No TrueType? 156
    Same-Name Fonts 157
    Reading Smoke Signals 157
    You Know You're Really in Trouble When. 159

7 Printing Pains 161
    Paths through Peril 161
    Choosy Printers 162
    Unavailable Printer 162
    Whose Fault? The Default Printer 163
    Dead Printer, Hardware-Wise 164
    Gray-Out Print Command 165

Dead Printer, Software-Wise 166
HP Printer Trouble 167
That's the Limit! 170
Bigger, BIGGER! 171
Out of Memory? Virtually. 171
Printing in Tongues 172
Half-Page Printing 173
The Big Printer Fake-Out 174
The Frozen Printer Era 175
Dead Print Screen 176
Likes DOS, Won't Do Windows! 177
ZZZZzzzzzz Printing 178
Reading Smoke Signals 178
You Know You're Really in Trouble When 180

8 Multimedia Horrors 181
Paths through Peril 181
The Invisible CD 182
Windows Doesn't C D CD 183
Spin-finity 184
Not Reading A (B) CD 185
Simple Sound Problems 186
Add Sound and You're Blasted 187
A Sound You Wish Were Silent 188
Unsupported Driver 190
Sound Locking 190
Hello, DOS? I Can't Hear You. 192
Are You a Player? 192
Did You Say Something? 193
Fried Multimedia Graphics 194
Slow-Motion Video 195
Reading Smoke Signals 196
You Know You're Really in Trouble When. 197

Table of Contents

9   Ready for Rescue: Memory Management 199
Paths through Peril 199
How Can I Be Out of Memory? 200
But I've Got 4MB! 201
A Mode by Any Other Name. 202
Pick a Mode, Any Mode 205
Mode Failure 206
How Do I Find Out What I've Got? 207
Slapped by the Swap File 209
TSR Trouble 211
Which Mode Is Which? 211
Loading Drivers: Oh No, I Won't! 212
RAM! I Need More RAM! 214
Reading Smoke Signals 214
You Know You're Really in Trouble When... 215

Epilogue 217
When Should You Call the Witch Doctor? 220
So, What Do the Scrolls Mean? 220

Index 229

Prologue

So, here you are again. First, it was the DOS fiasco, and now you're hanging on for dear life with this Windows thing. The witch doctor must be around here somewhere. Hope he's okay. He was on the ship with you when you left DOS Island, but now here you are overboard again. When will it end?

Floating out here on the sea of technology, you can get to daydreaming. . . .

Once upon a time, there was a canoe. Then someone attached an outboard motor to it, and it became a motor boat. The someone else — a computer programmer, no doubt — supercharged it and turned it into a state-of-the-art streamlined ski boat.

What? You don't like it? But it's faster. It does more. It's supposed to make your life easier.

But it's also lots more complicated, has more breakable parts, and is impossible to figure out in an afternoon.

Welcome to your own little corner of the computing world: Microsoft Windows. "Oh, it makes things easier," they said. "You'll learn it in no time," they insisted.

But things aren't working like they should. You're getting beeped at and seeing error messages and being assaulted by weird fonts. And someone keeps killing your mouse.

You are, as they say, up Windows Creek without a paddle.

Welcome to S.O.S. For Windows

Want to figure out your Windows problem and get back on the road to happy — or at least not-miserable — computing? Look through this book a little bit. *S.O.S. For Windows* includes quick, easy-to-get-to answers for those problems no one wants to help you with (or you're too embarrassed to ask).

S.O.S. For Windows helps pull you in to shore where you can investigate possible solutions or just plug the hole in the canoe — fast. And even though you'll find information on the biggest trouble spots — memory management, TrueType fonts, multimedia, and so on — you won't find yourself drowning in esoteric references that don't apply to your particular predicament.

Navigating through the Book

This isn't a book you'll read cover to cover. Who has time? When you're sinking, your only thought is "I'm sinking! How can I stop sinking?"

S.O.S. For Windows is organized so that you can find your problem easily and get right to the answer. You can look up your problem in the table of contents or the index and go right to that point in the book. For example, if

Prologue

you are trying to run a DOS program in Windows and it's giving you fits, turn to Chapter 5, "Devilish DOS Programs," to find possible solutions.

If you *do* decide to read this book from start to finish (got some time on your hands, eh?), you'll be able to follow the story line that accompanies the illustrations. You'll also notice the cool sidebars:

Techie Terms	Definitions of the most appalling computerese (words and phrases)
Witch Doctors	Suggestions on how to deal with technical support masters
Satchels	Recipes for making stuff to put in your satchel so that you will be better prepared in the future
Stepping Stones	Summarized steps for possible solutions

Smoke Signals	Error messages discussed nearby in the chapter
Words of Wisdom	Bits of witch doctor advice and extra tools you can use to enhance Windows
Road Signs	Warnings and directions to help you on your way
Scroll	Basic (but secret) troubleshooting tenets all the best witch doctors know

In the story line, you'll see the unfolding, heart-rending journey of one lost soul as he faces great adversity, struggling to survive in a land of confusion.

When You First Encounter Windows

You may have been watching with great trepidation as, one by one, your officemates started using Windows. You knew, sooner or later, that it would be your turn.

With great gnashing of teeth, you accept the mandate your company adopts: Everyone is switching to Windows. Yes, it's intimidating. Yes, you'd rather avoid it. But remember: Years from now, you'll look back on your anxieties and laugh.

When you first start using Windows, give yourself a break. Remember that you're working in a totally foreign environment — which is worse than just using a new program — so don't expect yourself to cope with everything perfectly.

People deal with stress in different ways: Good emotion-cleansing screams are one direct approach. Throwing your Windows manual or even swearing and making rude gestures at your monitor are within the realm of acceptability.

Prologue

7

But when you're really losing it, try not to physically assault your system. Knocking that laser printer off its stand is only going to hurt you — right in the pocketbook, too, where it hurts most.

In times of great stress, stand up and walk away. Go get yourself some M&Ms. And when the homicidal light has faded from your eyes, grab your copy of *S.O.S. For Windows* and start looking for your answer.

Part 1

What Happened? Where Am I?

After matching up with the witch doctor (and floating around for who knows how long), you finally spot land. Looks like another island. Better head for shore. Cold, bedraggled, and exhausted, you decide to swim for it nonetheless. But look at the witch doctor. He always seems to be better off. He looks so darned smug and comfortable. He says he'll take his time and just float that way. He'll catch up to you later. Yeah, sure — as long as there aren't any more hurricanes. . . .

Chapter 1

Off to a Bad Start

Paths through Peril

Talk about *trouble*. You thought sand crabs were a problem. And wet skivvies. But look at what's facing you now — installation, setup, startup ... oh, the horror of it all!

14

S.O.S. For Windows

My Computer Doesn't Work

Poison: A dead computer

They told you it would work. You were skeptical. First thing this morning, you walked into your office, gave that system a long, cold look to let it know who's boss, and flipped the power switch.

Nothing.

Not a flicker, not a beep. Not even an error message.

An overall dead computer is a ripe testing ground. The trouble could be caused by all kinds of things. Although computers do just die in their sleep from time to time, that is a rare occurrence and should be considered a last-case explanation.

Off to a Bad Start

Antidote: Ask yourself these questions:

- **Is the computer turned on?**

- **Is the computer's power cord plugged into the surge protector or into the wall?** Is the outlet working? Is the surge protector turned on and working?

- **Is your monitor the problem?** (Look for the power light on the front of your system unit. If the light is on, your computer is getting power.)

- **If you are using a laptop, is the battery charged?**

- **If you're on a network, is everyone else's computer down?** If everyone in your department is hooked up to the same network, and you're the only one with a dead screen, something is up with your system. If everyone is staring vacantly at a blank display, your network (and everyone in your department) may be temporarily out to lunch. If so, give your network administrator or your support desk a call.

WYSIN (What-You-See-Is-Nothing)

Poison: A blank monitor

You start up your computer and see nothing but a vast expanse of blankness displayed on the screen. Not a lot to work with.

Antidote:

- **Check for a power light.** (It's usually somewhere on the front of the monitor.) If the light is on, try adjusting the brightness and contrast controls (usually on the front or the side of the beast). If you still don't get a picture, check the back of your system to make sure that the monitor's video cable is connected to the system unit. And make sure that the system unit is turned on.

- **Make sure that your monitor is plugged in correctly.** Some monitors have their own power cords. Others plug into the back of the system unit, so you have two cables from the monitor to the system unit: one for power and one for the video signal.

- **Turn the monitor off, count to ten, and turn it back on.** While you do that, look in the top of the monitor to watch carefully for any signs of life (it could be that the little power light on the front is burned out). Listen, too. You'll be able to hear an electronic power-up noise if electric current is making its way into your monitor.

- **Connect the monitor to another computer system.** Does it work? If so, you isolated the problem: It's the system and not the monitor. If not, have your local witch doctor come and check things out.

Techie Term

RAM is an acronym for random-access memory, which is where your programs and data are stored while you're working with them.

Off to a Bad Start

17

What Does Windows Want from Me?

Poison: Lacking Windows essentials

You thought Windows would work on any IBM-type computer. You didn't know there were conditions. So you pushed the office manager into buying Windows 3.1 for the clunky old machines that you and the two other members of the support staff have to use every day. Now you're in a cold sweat. What if Windows doesn't work on your machines?

Antidote: The bare necessities for running Windows 3.1 on your computer are described on the box or in the manuals that come with the software. But, it's kind of like the government's minimum RDA for vitamins. Chances are, you need to go out and buy more RAM, a bigger hard disk, and the best processor money can buy. (And please, get a mouse.) If you want all the bells and whistles, you may also want to invest in a nice laser printer, a modem, sound board, or CD-ROM.

Okay, Let's Go!

Poison: Over-eager installers

You're ready to get it over with. Face the installation music and all that. But hold on a minute — let's think this through.

Off to a Bad Start

Rushing into installation without advance planning is like diving blindfolded into the sea from a hundred-foot cliff. You're very likely to hit your head on the rocks below, and it may take you a long time to surface again.

Antidote: Before you install Windows, do the following:

- Back up everything on your hard drive. (For specific information on how to do backups, see *DOS For Dummies*.)

- Create a Survival Disk if you haven't already done so (see the satchel sidebar in this chapter).

- Make another safety disk and put copies of your AUTOEXEC.BAT and CONFIG.SYS files on it.

S.O.S. For Windows

- Delete any unnecessary programs and files on your hard disk to free up more room for Windows.

- Use a diagnostics program such as Norton Disk Doctor or DOS 6.2's new ScanDisk feature to make sure that everything is cool on your hard disk. (If you prefer, you can use the DOS command CHKDSK /F instead.)

- Make sure that you don't have any TSRs loaded. (Not sure? Watch for suspicious fly-by messages when you reboot.) If you have DOS 6.2, you can bypass your AUTOEXEC.BAT and CONFIG.SYS files (which automatically load various drivers and may load your TSRs without you knowing it) by pressing F5 when you see the message `Starting MS-DOS...`"

- Make copies of your original Windows program disks and use the copies to install the program. (Put the originals away in their box and store them somewhere safe.)

Techie Term

TSR is an acronym for terminate-and-stay-resident, which describes a type of program that goes on working behind the scenes while you work on other things. One popular TSR includes an alarm clock that pops up over your current program when you press a certain key or when it's time to go to lunch.

Pretty Hefty Program!

Poison: Short on free space

Someone told you once that Windows was a big program. You thought that the reference was to the program's popularity. Now, as you're getting

Off to a Bad Start

ready to install it, you find out that Windows is *big* in terms of the storage space it eats up.

But 10MB is not such a big deal when you've got a 120MB hard drive, you say.

You're right. But after you install Windows, you're likely to use other Windows programs, such as WordPerfect for Windows, Microsoft PowerPoint, or Excel. Add another 15 to 20MB for each additional Windows program.

Racking it up, aren't we?

Antidote: Before you begin to install Windows, look carefully through your hard disk and delete any unnecessary programs and data. Be sure to back up your hard disk before you start deleting things, though.

Note: You may want to use a disk compression program, such as DOS 6.0's DoubleSpace or Stacker, to squish the data on your hard drive into a smaller space. If you don't feel totally comfortable making big changes on your hard drive, ask the witch doctor for advice. (Or consult *S.O.S. For DOS* from IDG for additional assistance.)

Crawling Installing

Poison: A slow boat to nowhere

Windows is installing very slowly. It's agony. You watch as the status line creeps across the screen and the light stays on and on and on.

Antidote: You may have a disk problem. Installation should move along at a pretty good pace and take a total of 10 to 15 minutes. (On some machines, it can take a lot longer.) Make sure you have an uncluttered hard drive. And make sure it's healthy. Find a witch doctor and throw some terms at him, such as defragment, ScanDisk, CHKDSK, COMPRESS, diagnostics program, and so on.

How to Make a Windows System Disk

Witch doctors know which tools to use in a crisis. One of the most basic tools is the System Disk — the disk that gets you out of trouble once trouble troubles you.

If you are using a computer with a hard drive, you're accustomed to having everything start just the way it's supposed to. But someday you may find that your computer forgets the routine.

That's when the System Disk comes in handy.

The System Disk is a disk that has — already on it — the commands your computer needs in order to start. How come the commands are already on there? You put them there, by starting the File Manager, opening the Disk menu, choosing Format Disk, and clicking the Make System Disk checkbox.

After you click OK, Windows then formats the disk and adds the necessary system commands. Make sure you label the disk so you can tell — under pressure — which one can save you from your plight.

You may be so relieved that you'll be tempted to make dozens of System Disks — just to be safe. A couple more aren't a bad idea, but *dozens* might be overdoing it.

What Is a Witch Doctor?

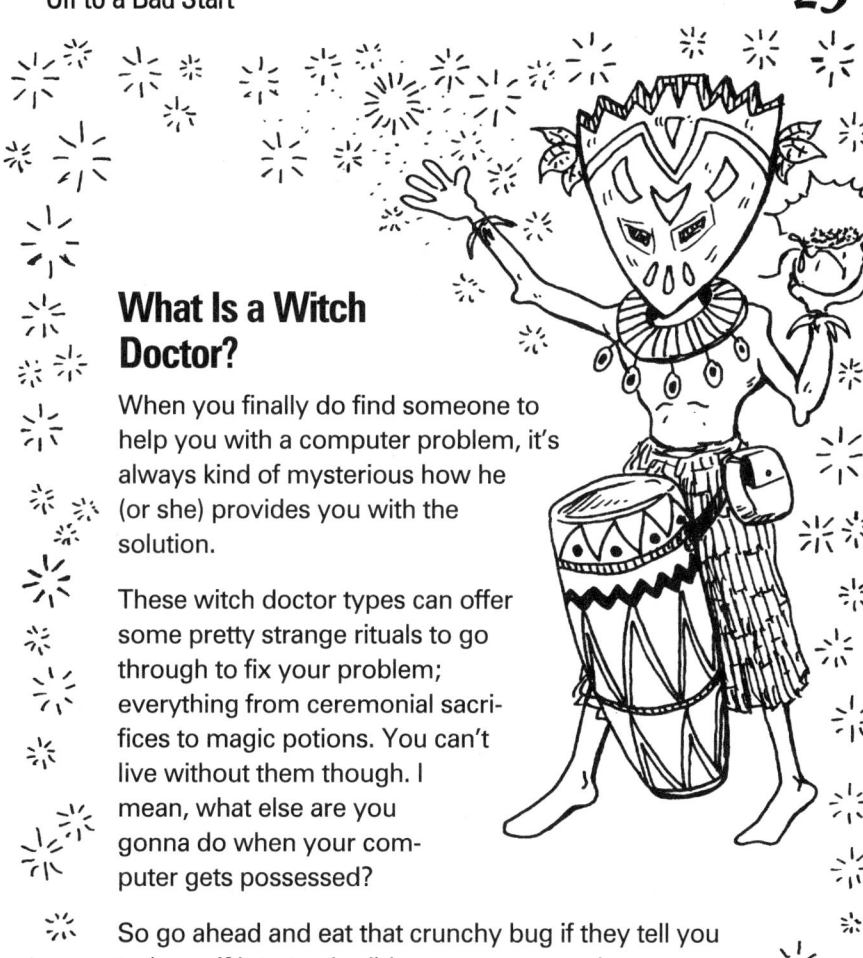

When you finally do find someone to help you with a computer problem, it's always kind of mysterious how he (or she) provides you with the solution.

These witch doctor types can offer some pretty strange rituals to go through to fix your problem; everything from ceremonial sacrifices to magic potions. You can't live without them though. I mean, what else are you gonna do when your computer gets possessed?

So go ahead and eat that crunchy bug if they tell you to (even if it tastes bad) because you may have no other choice. Before you do though, make sure that you've found a true witch doctor (there are lots of quacks you know). To learn how to find a good one, see Chapter 2.

For additional advice about how to facilitate your interactions with witch doctors (and hopefully increase the chances of solving your problem), look for these witch doctor sidebars throughout the book.

24

S.O.S. For Windows

Sleuthing Screwy Setups

Poison: A Setup hanging

You started out all right. You made it though the DOS portion of Setup and saw the Windows opening screen. Files were copying. Things were moving. And then . . . lockup.

Antidote: Find out the answer to each of these questions:

- **What version of DOS are you using?**
  (For best results, you should be using DOS 3.1 or later.)

- **Do you have any TSRs loaded?**
  TSRs don't make Windows happy — especially at installation. Some TSRs go away when you reboot the computer; others are loaded in AUTOEXEC.BAT (watch for on-screen messages) and will come back unless you edit AUTOEXEC.BAT. Before you make any changes to AUTOEXEC.BAT, consult your witch doctor.

- **Does your AUTOEXEC.BAT file have this line:**

    SET TEMP=C:\TEMP

  Windows needs the TEMP directory in order to operate properly.

- **Does your CONFIG.SYS file set FILES=40?**
  Your system will need plenty of room while it's working with

Techie Term

Driver is a special type of program. A *video driver*, for example, is a program that tells other programs how to work with your monitor and graphics card. A *printer driver* contains information about the printer. A *mouse driver* runs important mouse stuff. You get the idea.

Windows, and this line expands some boundaries to their necessary limits.

Note: When you make it all the way through installation (and you will, eventually), Windows will ask you whether it's okay to go ahead and modify both your AUTOEXEC.BAT and CONFIG.SYS files to include the necessary settings. Let it do so.

What Kind of Monitor Is That?

Poison: Unconventional video driver

When you're running Setup, you notice that your monitor isn't included in the Windows list of monitor options. Does that mean that Windows won't work or that it will look strange when it does?

Antidote: Windows determines what type of monitor it "thinks" you have during the initial phase of Setup. In most cases, the screen display will be fine if you let Windows continue thinking that it chose the right display. To make sure you've got the best possible display, however, contact your monitor's manufacturer to get the most current video driver.

What Kind of Printer Is That?

Poison: Unknown printer

When you reach the moment of installing a printer driver, the choices can seem pretty overwhelming. Windows shows you an exhaustive list of the million and one printers it supports.

And yours isn't on the list.

Antidote: If you can't find your printer on the list, you can do several things:

- Call the printer manufacturer (or Microsoft) to get the most recent driver for your particular printer.

- **Install a printer driver for a printer that's the same brand and nearly the same style as the one you're using.** I once installed a printer driver for a QMS PS 410 when I had a PS 810, and the printing was just fine.

- **Install a printer driver for a printer that's similar to yours but isn't the same brand.** For example, many dot-matrix printers can *emulate* (act like) an Epson printer, so if you choose an Epson printer driver, your printouts may be A-OK. (If you choose a driver and your printouts aren't A-OK, you can always go back to the Printers box in the Control Panel and select a different driver.)

- **Install the Generic/Text printer driver.**

Appalling Reinstalling

Poison: Reinstall problems

You've just reinstalled Windows to a different directory on your hard disk (Why? Because you're a glutton for punishment.) Now Windows won't run.

Antidote: If Setup went okay (meaning you didn't get any weird error messages and didn't smell smoke), you know the cause of the Windows weirdness is one of these things:

- **Did you say No when Windows asked to make changes to the PATH statement in AUTOEXEC.BAT?** Windows inserts the C:\WINDOWS; statement in your PATH line so you can start Windows from any directory.

- **Did you delete any Windows files from the directory in an attempt to conserve space?**

- **Do you have enough conventional memory to run Windows?**

- **One of your Windows files may be corrupted.** Although if this were the case, you probably would have seen some kind of error message when Setup copied over the necessary files.

Off to a Bad Start

Windows No Like TSRs

Poison: TSR trouble message

Right after you knuckle in and start Windows installation, you get a beep and a message that you've got a TSR running that could trip Windows up.

Words of Wisdom:

Control Panel

Half the secret of being a witch doctor is knowing where to find the things you need. The Control Panel, in the Main group, is the place where you set up all your stuff to work with Windows.

In the Control Panel, you control screen colors, set up and remove fonts, choose your ports, control your mouse and keyboard, make decisions about the way your desktop looks, set up printers, sound devices, install various drivers, and specify settings like the language you use and the date and time. Whenever you add a new something to your computer (like a printer or sound card) or beef up your font library, make a trip to the Control Panel.

About Program Manager

The About Program Manager option, in the Help menu, tells you what Windows mode you're running and tells you how much memory you have to run it.

> **Important DOS Files**
> Two important DOS files — AUTOEXEC.BAT and CONFIG.SYS — are also important to Windows. They contain instructions and settings your computer needs at startup.

What the heck's a TSR and how did it get on your system? And even more important, what do you do about it?

Antidote: The Setup program automatically looks for any terminate-and-stay-resident programs that could give the installation utility problems. But, as intelligent as Windows is, it can't see every possible type of TSR.

- If you loaded the TSR yourself by typing a command at the DOS prompt before you started Windows, you can remove it by exiting Setup, rebooting your computer (press Ctrl+Alt+Del), and restarting Setup without starting the TSR.

- If you didn't load anything and don't have the foggiest notion what a TSR is, ask the local witch doctor to help. You could try looking for the TSR yourself (it is loaded automatically in your AUTOEXEC.BAT file), but sometimes it's better to pull up short than to go chasing maybes.

Note: For more information on the Windows-and-TSRs thing, see Chapter 9.

Off to a Bad Start

Incompatible Differences

Poison: Windows-unfriendly commands

During Setup, Windows displays a message that incompatible commands have been found in your AUTOEXEC.BAT file. Incompatible commands? Like what? GO and STOP? WORK and LIVE? WALK and CHEWGUM?

Antidote: There are several DOS commands that Windows doesn't especially like. And if Setup finds them in your AUTOEXEC.BAT file, its going to cross it's arms and say "Nuh uh." Open AUTOEXEC.BAT and look for these commands:

APPEND	JOIN
FASTOPEN	PRINT
GRAPHICS	SHARE

If you find any of these culprits, remove them. (Make a copy of the AUTOEXEC.BAT file first — just in case you need it later.)

Then go skipping back into Setup and try the whole thing over again.

Note: For the real scoop on how to edit your AUTOEXEC.BAT and CONFIG.SYS files as safely as possible (don't forget those latex gloves), see *DOS For Dummies*, by Dan Gookin (IDG, 1993).

Setup also checks the list of incompatible drivers in SETUP.INF. If any of these incompatible drivers are listed in CONFIG.SYS or if the MS-DOS APPEND, SUBST, or JOIN commands are in AUTOEXEC.BAT, Setup displays a message box explaining that incompatible drivers or commands have been found. Also, Setup checks the FILES= entry in CONFIG.SYS to make sure that the number of file handles is at least 30.

Note: Many of the problems that occur at startup have to do with low memory. For more information on fixing memory glitches, see Chapter 9.

You Just Can't WIN

Poison: Windows isn't there.

You followed the directions. You did all the right things. You typed **WIN** and pressed Enter and your computer screamed

```
Bad command or file name
```

Antidote: In times of great duress, checklists are a big help:

- Are you in the WINDOWS (or WIN) directory?
- Do you know where your Windows directory is?
- Are you sure that Windows is installed? (Do a DIR or a TREE of your hard disk to see whether you have a WINDOWS directory.)
- Is Windows in your PATH statement?
- Do you need to type a different command sequence to start Windows on your system? (Talk to your company's witch doctor to make sure.)
- Did you type the startup command (WIN) correctly? (Press F3 to display what you just typed.)

No-Go Windows

Poison: Windows won't start.

You worked through the checklist and discovered that you really do have Windows. It just won't start.

Antidote: First, check these things:

- Are any other programs running while you're trying to run Windows? If you're not sure, reboot and watch the screen. A TSR will display a message when it loads. Examine AUTOEXEC.BAT if necessary.

Off to a Bad Start

- **Do you have enough memory?** (Use the DOS MEM command to determine how much memory you have. Realistically, your computer needs 1MB for Standard mode and 2MB for 386 Enhanced mode.)

- **Do you have two important files — WIN.INI and SYSTEM.INI — in your WINDOWS directory?**

- **Do you have a file named HIMEM.SYS in either your WINDOWS or your root directory?** Search both directories for *.SYS to find out. Windows needs this file to resolve some memory issues.

- **Does your CONFIG.SYS have a line that says**

    ```
    DEVICE=C:\WINDOWS\HIMEM.SYS
    ```

    The drive and directory will be different than the ones shown here, of course, if your version of Windows is stored in a different drive and directory.

If you check all these things and everything looks A-OK, try forcing Windows to start in standard mode. Enter the following command at the DOS prompt:

```
WIN /S
```

If Windows is going to start, it will after you enter this command. If Windows is dug in to give you trouble, contact your witch doctor. It may be that Windows guessed wrong when it tried to identify your hardware during installation. If so, some technical things need to be straightened out. You can look over the witch doctor's shoulder (and perhaps run to the candy machine for backup M&Ms), but don't try doing major Setup renovation yourself.

Headache A La Mode

Poison: Mode confusion

You don't know what mode to start Windows in.

Antidote: Let Windows do the thinking for you. In most cases, Windows will sense what kind of system you have and start your computer the right way.

However, you should "force" Windows to start in a certain mode in two situations:

- When you're getting `Out of Memory` errors or when Windows won't start, try starting Windows in standard mode. Just type **WIN /S** at the DOS prompt and press Enter.

- When your system is supposed to be running in 386 enhanced mode and it's running in standard mode, try forcing Windows into 386 mode. Type **WIN /3** at the DOS prompt and press Enter.

Note: For more information on using standard and 386 enhanced modes, see Chapter 9.

Maybe I Will, Maybe I Won't

Poison: Windows starts and hangs.

Off to a Bad Start

Oh, you thought you had it. The light came on. The system started making that "chunk, chunk" sound. The Windows opening screen came up and then . . .

Major lockup.

The on-screen pointer (that little arrow) doesn't move when you move the mouse. You push a few keys and nothing happens. You look in your manual for advice on how to open a menu (press the Alt key and the underlined letter in the menu name) and try it. Nothing.

Antidote: The culprit can be several things:

- Not enough memory (use a memory optimizer such as MEMMAKER to make the most of your available RAM)
- Wrong hardware installation
- Missing or corrupted program files

Tackle the problem by following these steps:

1. Reboot your computer and watch for error messages.

2. Type **MEM** or **CHKDSK** at the DOS prompt and see how much available memory you have.

3. If you have enough memory, try starting Windows in Standard mode (type **WIN /S**).

4. If you get into Windows, try opening the Main window (double-click on its icon) and then double-clicking on the Windows Setup icon. A small box appears to show you what type of system Windows thinks you have.

Having the wrong display installed — for example, if you have an EGA display but Windows installed a VGA driver — can cause some weird Windows problems. Look for inconsistencies and make any necessary changes.

If Windows got the big items wrong — system unit stuff such as available memory — you need the witch doctor's special magic. Fight the temptation to reduce your system to the electronic dust from whence it came and get out that witch doctor whistle.

Time-Warp Windows

Problem: Really, *really* sloooooow

You made it through the startup perils, but something's fishy. *How* long did it take the Microsoft Windows opening screen to appear?

Words of Wisdom: MEMMAKER

If you have DOS 6 and a 386 or 486 machine, use MEMMAKER (an automatic memory optimizer utility) to make the most of your available memory. Just exit to DOS (if you're not already there), and type

    MEMMAKER

After you press Enter, you'll see a number of things on-screen. Don't panic. For the most part, MEMMAKER will take care of things for you. When MEMMAKER is through, it gives you instructions on restarting your program and tells you how much memory it has saved you. Now you should have more elbow room in RAM.

Every time you make major changes to your system configuration (such as adding more memory or other hardware), run MEMMAKER again to update it.

Off to a Bad Start

Antidote: The most common cause of molasses-like Windows operation is an insufficient amount of memory. Sure, you may have the amount of memory that the Windows box said you needed: 1MB. But if you really want to do anything with any kind of speed, you'll be much better off with 2MB. Most Windows enthusiasts wouldn't think of running Windows with less than 4MB. (Good thing we're not Windows enthusiasts.)

Short of upgrading your memory right away, you can try a few other things:

- Make sure that you don't have any other programs loaded that could be eating up memory.

- Make sure that you're running in the right mode. If Windows is painfully slow, try forcing it to run in standard mode by using the startup command WIN /S. Even on most 386 systems, standard mode seems to operate faster. It may make a difference on your system or it may not. But it's worth typing a few characters to find out.

- Use a memory manager, such as 386MAX or DOS's EMM386.EXE memory manager, to make the most of your available memory.

- Make sure that there aren't any TSRs that load automatically and eat up memory (check AUTOEXEC.BAT to find out).

- Find out whether your system is loading anything — even certain device drivers — that you may not need.

Here It Comes Again!

Poison: Unwanted automatic Windows

Windows just pops merrily up on your screen every time you start that blasted computer. You don't want it there.

Antidote: Use Notepad or Windows Write to open your AUTOEXEC.BAT file. (Make a copy of it first and name it something like AUTOEXEC.OLD.) Look for the line that just says WIN. Put the cursor in front of it and type **REM** and press the spacebar. Now save the file.

The next time you start your computer (whether you reboot or turn the thing off and on), Windows should be gone (until you summon it, of course).

Where Is It?

Poison: Not there when you want it

Everyone else gets to come in to work, push the power button on the computer, and have their software come up automatically. But not you. For you, it's just that mean-looking DOS prompt and the impatient cursor (blink, blink, blink).

Antidote: Just add a line to your AUTOEXEC.BAT file to make the magic happen. Make a copy of AUTOEXEC.BAT (rename it something else) and open the file in Notepad. Take a look at your PATH statement to make sure there's an entry that says C:\WINDOWS; (or D:\WINDOWS if your copy is on drive D). Now move the cursor to the bottom of the file and type **WIN**. Save the file and close it. The next time you punch that power button, Windows should come rushing into view.

Note: If your friend has Windows come up automatically and then has other programs open automatically *in Windows* (that's a lot of automaticallys), it's because she's put those programs in her Startup group. For more about adding your own programs to the Startup group, see *Windows For Dummies*, by Andy Rathbone (IDG 1992).

Off to a Bad Start

The Case of the Dead Mouse

Poison: Belly-up mouse

Windows is so great because you can use your mouse to point-and-click your way to true User Happiness, right? Well, your mouse is history.

Antidote: First — don't panic. It's probably something simple. Let's narrow it down:

- Has the mouse worked in other applications? (If the mouse worked with a DOS program, for example, you know it works.)

- Have you changed anything in your system (added a sound board, put in a modem) that could be conflicting with the mouse?

- Did you install a driver for your mouse during the Windows installation process?

- Do you have a non-Microsoft mouse? If so, your mouse driver may cause problems, and you should call your witch doctor for help.

Mouse-Cicles

Poison: Mouse freezes everything

Ah — there it is. The Program Manager. Sweet success.

You click on the Games icon and play a few hands of Solitaire. You click on the word processor and type a letter. You're having a high old time opening things and playing and printing and moving and then . . .

Hey. What's this? The mouse is stuck. You look up instructions on how to use the keyboard to open a menu (you're looking in *Windows For Dummies*, right?). You press Alt and the appropriate underlined letter, like the instructions say.

Nothing. Your computer is locked up.

Antidote: If this is the first time your mouse has locked your system up, shut everything off and turn it back on. Go back to your application. Sometimes things like this just happen. But if this is a recurring nightmare, you may need a simple fix in a line in CONFIG.SYS.

If you have DOS 3.2 or later, you can solve the problem by adding the following line to your CONFIG.SYS file:

```
STACKS=9,256
```

This instruction sets the number of stacks to 9 and the size of each stack to 256 bytes.

Whenever you move the mouse (which is quite a bit), click a mouse button, or type on the keyboard, a signal is sent to the microprocessor in your computer. This signal is called an *interrupt* (it interrupts normal processing).

DOS can only deal with so many interrupts at a time. When it gets more interrupts than it can handle, it starts stacking them up. The piles of interrupts are called *stacks*. If DOS doesn't have enough stacks to hold the interrupts, it throws up its hands and says "What's the use?" The result? Your computer locks up.

One Blind Mouse

Poison: A stuck mouse pointer

This problem is likely to occur the first time you try to use the mouse with Windows. You type **WIN**, and the Program Manager appears. The mouse pointer is right in the middle of the screen. You try to move it by moving the mouse. The mouse moves, but the pointer doesn't.

Antidote: You need to ask yourself a few questions:

- Are you sure that the mouse is plugged into the back of the system unit?

Off to a Bad Start

- **Are your mouse drivers installed?** (Do you have either MOUSE.SYS or MOUSE.COM? Did Windows install either MOUSE.DRV or HPMOUSE.DRV?)

- **Does the mouse work outside of Windows?** Try the mouse with your favorite "I-know-it-works" DOS program.

Nuttin' Doin'

Poison: An unresponsive keyboard

You press a key and nothing happens. You press Esc. Nothing. You type WAKEUP! Nothing.

Antidote: The problem could be several things:

- **Is the keyboard plugged into the system unit?**

- **Have you spilled anything in it lately (like a glass of Cabernet)?**

- **Did you "lose" the keyboard when you started Windows?**

- **Can you use the keyboard from DOS?** (Turn your computer off, count to ten, and turn it back on.)

If your keyboard works okay when you use DOS but not when you're in Windows, you may have the wrong keyboard installed. In that case, open Windows Setup and if your keyboard type isn't listed, open the Options menu and select Change System Settings to select the one you use.

This Looks Awful!

Poison: Display problems

You've gone through all this agony and finally started Windows up. But just look at it! How are you supposed to use a distorted, rolling picture like that?

Antidote: The most obvious problem is your graphics driver. Did you install the right driver for your display, or did you make a lucky guess? Windows goes out and makes a best-guess for you, so if you changed the default setting, rerun Setup (exit Windows and type **Setup** at the DOS prompt in the WINDOWS directory) and let Windows reselect its first choice for display adapter.

If, when you return to Windows, you still have the same problem, try Setup again and choose a lower-grade driver. If you still have trouble, contact the manufacturer to see whether there's a later version of your graphics driver you've missed.

Note: Wait! Put down that club! For more information on deciphering your hardware (before it deciphers you), see *Upgrading & Fixing PCs For Dummies*, by Andy Rathbone (IDG, 1993).

Reading Smoke Signals

The first leg of your journey can be a scary one. Remember that if your system comes on at all, it's a good sign. There's life in there somewhere. Now you just have to figure out what your computer is telling you. Here are a few messages you might see if your system is having install, setup, or startup trouble:

Error in CONFIG.SYS, line 8

Your computer clunked and whirred its way past the POST test. It flashed a number of lines on the screen too quickly for you to read. An encouraging sign. Everything seems to be loading normally, until you get an error message. Your *operating system* is telling you that it's hanging up on a certain line in an important file your computer uses at startup, CONFIG.SYS. Insert your System Disk in drive A, reboot your computer by pressing Ctrl+Alt+Del, and then try to tackle the problem.

Internal stack overflow

A *stack* is a pile where *interrupts* are stored. What's an interrupt? Every time you press a key on the keyboard or click a mouse button, the action sends

You must have WINA20.386

POST ERROR Code 1102

Out of Memory

Keyboard error, press F2 to continue

Internal stack overflow

Error in CONFIG.SYS, line 8

data streaming through your computer. Chances are, your computer is totally locked up and your only recourse is to reboot. But that's okay — sounds like your stacks needed a little cleaning.

Keyboard error, press F2 to continue

Most likely, your keyboard isn't plugged into the back of the system unit. Make sure that the cord isn't crimped. Then follow it around to the keyboard port (that's where the cable plugs in). Make sure that everything is plugged in tightly and reboot your computer.

Out of Memory

If you get an Out of Memory message, you may wonder how your system can be out of RAM when you've got beaucoup megabytes free. This error message, which you may see with either Windows 3.0 or 3.1, is really about graphical user memory. What can you do? Try closing a few windows.

POST ERROR Code 1102

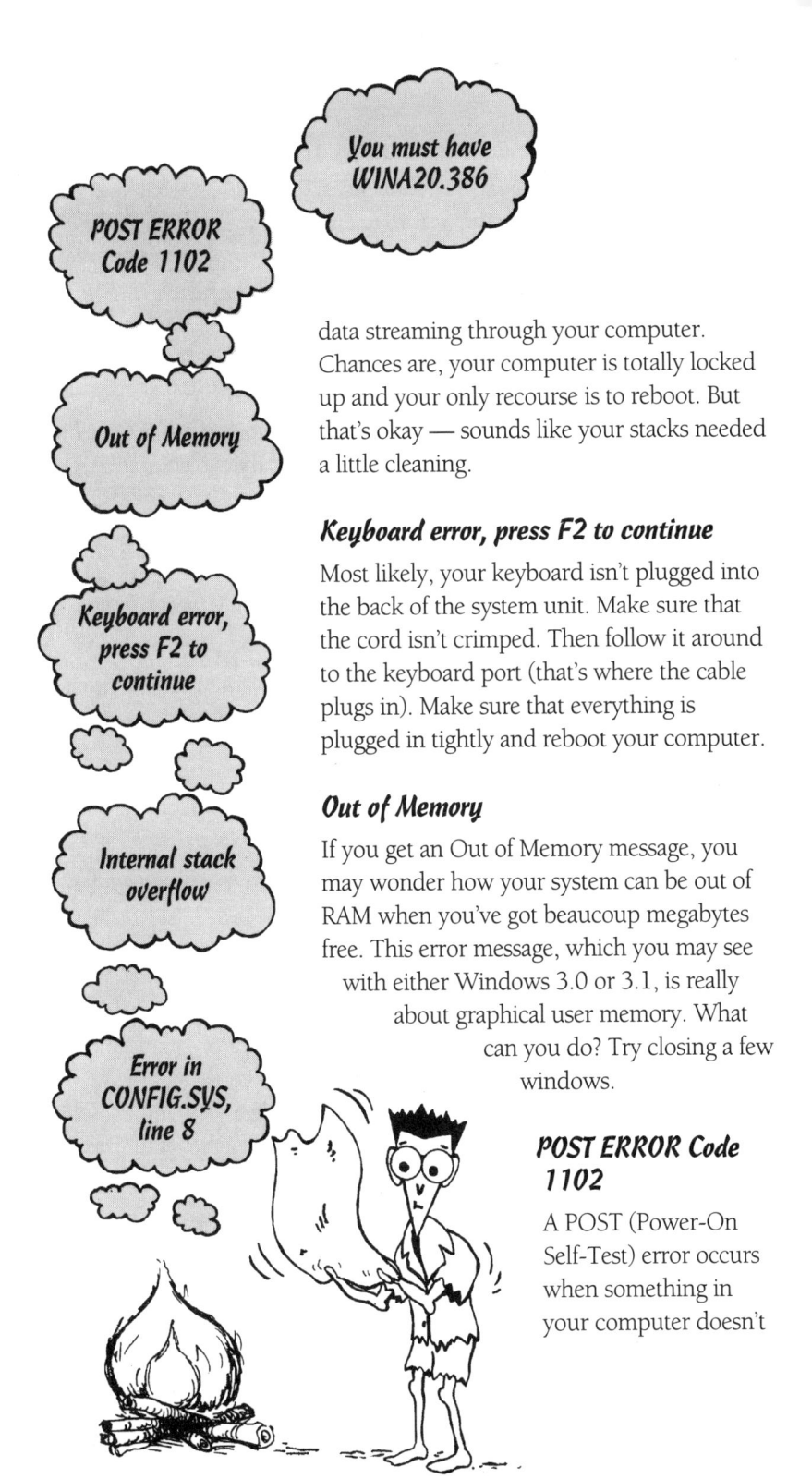

A POST (Power-On Self-Test) error occurs when something in your computer doesn't pass the initial tests your computer performs on itself. POST errors are often accompanied by strange beep sequences. Write down what you see (or just leave it displayed on the screen) and contact your witch doctor.

You must have WINA20.386 in the root directory of the drive you booted from

You can tell that this is a Windows error message; you'd never get this much explanation from DOS. (And it's a version 3.0 error, not 3.1, by the way.) You're trying to run Windows in 386 enhanced mode, and one of the files that Windows needs — WINA20.386 — isn't where it should be. Do a directory of the disk you use to start your computer (usually drive C: or D:) to see whether WINA20.386 is there. Get to the root directory (that would be C:\) and type

```
DIR *.386
```

If the file isn't where is should be, reinstall it from your Windows program disk (use EXPAND, not COPY, to place the file in your WINDOWS directory).

You Know You're Really in Trouble When...

You accidentally delete your WIN.INI file

Hmmm. Housecleaning again? Any time you see an .INI file, keep it: it's a special file Windows uses for setting things up. Different programs and elements can have their own .INI files. Windows uses those files to keep tabs on the various devices in your system. If you delete WIN.INI and don't have a backup, you really *are* in trouble. Chances are, you're looking at a total reinstall of Windows (and possibly your other applications as well). Call your witch doctor to help you.

Your system doesn't have enough memory to run Windows

If you tried everything (like getting someone to help you use a memory manager) and then some (like using DOS 6.0's MEMMAKER utility), and you still don't have enough memory, you may as well give up on Windows until someone okays a memory upgrade.

Chapter 2

Program Manager Perils

Paths through Peril

Feeling more on top of things? Don't relax yet — Program Manager problems are on the way. And if that isn't bad enough, you've got to wrestle all those little windows into submission and show them who's boss. . . .

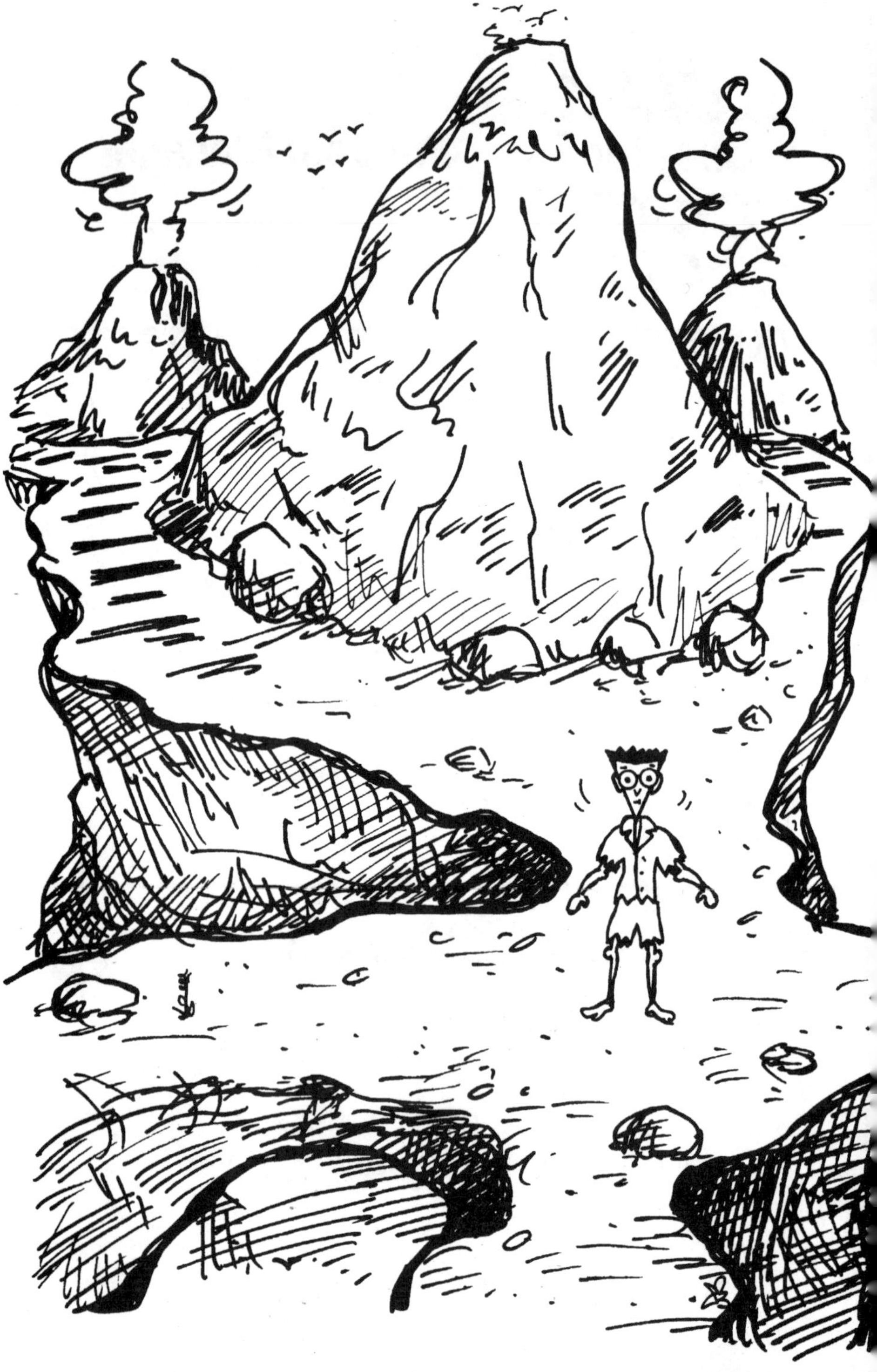

Program Manager Lite

Poison: Teeny tiny Program Manager

You start up Windows, and you see this gray screen with an itsy bitsy picture in the bottom left corner. Get out your magnifying glass. *That's* the Program Manager? The great and powerful Program Manager? It's just a little icon.

Someone has done a nice thing and cleaned your Windows desktop for you. If you prefer, you can open the Program Manager window and make sure that it stays open by following a couple of simple steps.

Antidote: First, double-click on the Program Manager icon to open the Program Manager. See? There it is. Before you do anything else, open the Options menu. Click on the Save Settings on Exit option so that a check mark appears beside it.

Now, run any programs you need to run and go about your business. After you finish your work, but before you exit Windows, make sure that the Program Manager remains open. Then when you start Windows in the morning, the Program Manager should be just the way you left it.

See . . .

Just when you think you're safe, a volcano erupts, and you're on the run again.

In Windows 3.1, there's quicker fix: Just get the display the way you want it, press Shift and Ctrl and double-click the Program Manager's control menu box in the upper left corner of the window. Too cool.

Short, Fat Program Manager

Poison: Distorted display

Funny, your Program Manager is shorter and squatter than you expected it to be on-screen. You look over the cubicle wall at your coworker's screen. Hmmm. Hers isn't scrunched like yours.

Antidote: The way you fix this depends on how bad your screen looks. If you can make out what's going on — it just looks strange — you can change the graphics card selected in Windows Setup. Just go to the Windows Setup group in the Main window, double-click it, and choose Add/Change System Components.

But if the display is so distorted that you really can't tell what's what, you need to exit Windows, go to the DOS prompt in the WINDOWS directory, and type Setup. That will take you back in to the Setup program so you can reinstall the correct graphics card.

Spots Before Your Eyes

Poison: Tiny wallpaper

Your coworkers have cool backgrounds (known in Windows as *wallpaper*) on their Windows screens: keep-you-awake kinds of backgrounds with wild colors and panache. All you have is a Windows logo, smack dab in the middle of the screen. And as soon as the Program Manager opens, it covers up the logo.

Antidote: Your wallpaper is stuck in the center of your screen instead of being spread out to the edges of your display. Change that in the Desktop

Program Manager Perils

window (that's the Control Panel, by the way). Just change Center to Tile and you're in business.

Clashing Colors

Poison: Eye-strain colors

By default, Windows sets itself up to be on the conservative side with screen color. So if you want to impress Reba from the art department with your creative use of screen colors, you have to make some changes.

Antidote: To change the screen colors, open the Main window and double-click on the Control Panel. Choose Color (the first icon) and let the creative juices flow.

You can choose one of many color schemes by clicking on the down arrow at the end of the Color Schemes box. (Designer is cool; Hotdog Stand will wake you up; and Wingtips is for, well, people who wear wing-tipped shoes). If you prefer, you can create your own color scheme from scratch by clicking on the Color Palette button and choosing a color for each screen element. The display box shows you what you're choosing as you go along. (You're not one of those people who mixes pink and red, are you? In that case, you're much better off choosing one of Windows' own prefab color schemes. Trust me!)

Now Entering the Screen Saver Zone

Poison: Seeing stars

You're sitting at your desk after a visit from the witch doctor, who just installed Windows. It appears to be working fine, and you're on your own. A little nervous, of course, you reach up to move the mouse, when. . .

You see stars — not just a couple of stars, but many of them — coming right at you. What's happened to your computer?

Antidote: The witch doctor forgot to tell you that he installed a *screen saver*, a program that keeps your monitor from burning in elements that are continually displayed. Windows 3.1 comes with five different screen saver utilities. If you're seeing stars, then you have Starfield Simulation on-screen right now.

To return to Windows, do anything: move the mouse, press a key. Windows comes back right away. To change how long Windows waits before starting the screen saver, open the Desktop window and change the Screen Saver settings.

Fool-Safe Screen Saving

Poison: Screen saver that wouldn't die

When you move the mouse or press a key to get rid of the screen saver, the following message appears:

```
The screen saver you are using is password protected. You
must type in the screen saver password to turn off the
screen saver.
```

Password? *What* password?

Antidote: The situation isn't as bad as you think. You *will* be able to use your computer again. However, right now, you have to reboot your computer. (Hopefully, you've saved what you were working on most recently.)

When you restart Windows, get to the Screen Saver section of the Desktop window. Click the Setup button and another dialog box appears. Beside the Password Protected option is a check box with an X in it. Click inside the box to remove the X. Now your screen saver isn't password protected. Click on OK (and OK again) to get out of the Desktop settings.

Disappearing Program Groups

Poison: Missing groups

A new employee's nightmare: You walk into the office, ready to face Windows; you power up, sit down, and then — face an empty Program Manager.

No, an empty Program Manager doesn't mean you have nothing to do all day. It means something (or someone) has blown away or corrupted your program groups.

Discovering a missing program group (one or all) is a terrifying experience because users often think that if the icon is gone, the program is gone. Remember that the icon is just the button that leads to the program (such as the on/off knob somebody pulled off the old Zenith). The program (or the TV) is still there, but you need to get another button.

Antidote: Lucky for you, the wizards at Microsoft predicted that this nightmare may happen some time. They even built in a command specifically for rebuilding program groups that we mere mortals blow away. The command is SETUP /P and it rebuilds all the default program groups Windows starts with. But what about the ones you've added? Looks like you'll be setting those back up yourself.

Simply choose the Run command from the File menu and type **SETUP /P**. Then click on OK or press Enter and go get a Coke while Windows does the work.

Techie Term

A *program item* is one of those little icons inside the group window that can actually start a program. You can add or delete program items to group windows (which doesn't mean that you are adding or deleting the actual program).

But then — sorry — you have to get back to work (or at least to playing Minesweeper).

Go Nowhere Icons

Poison: Icon doesn't like directory

You opened the correct group window and found the icon you're looking for: the Microsoft Word 6.0 icon. You put the mouse pointer on the icon and double-click. The following message appears:

```
The working directory is invalid.
```

Now what do you do?

Antidote: There are two possible explanations for your problem:

- Someone (maybe you) has deleted the program.
- Someone (maybe you) has moved the program.

Windows is looking for the program in the place where it used to be, but it is not finding the program. Click on OK to remove the error box. (If you see another error box, click on OK again.) Position the mouse pointer on the icon in question and press Alt while double-clicking. The Program Item Properties dialog box appears.

Write down the information in the Command Line and Working Directory text boxes. Then click on the Browse button. Click on the Directories box to find the subdirectory for the missing (or moved) program. The program's filename will end with .EXE, .COM, or .BAT.

If the program has been moved to another location, correct the Command Line and Working Directory entries and then click on OK. If the program has been deleted, either remove the program item or reinstall the program.

Program Manager Perils **51**

Attack of the Weirdo Icons

Poison: Annoying icons

Did you change the look of your icons like the *Windows For Dummies* book told you to? (Maybe somebody changed your icons while you were out to lunch.) Because some programs (especially DOS programs) aren't real creative with their choices for program icons, Windows gives you alternative icons in the PROGMAN.EXE and MORICONS.DLL files. (Without a specific icon, Windows just shows you a boring icon that says MS-DOS.)

Antidote: To get rid of the icons that you've got (or change them to something else), press the Alt key and double-click on the icon you want to change. The Program Item Properties dialog box appears. A little picture of the current icon appears in the lower left corner. Click on the Change Icon button and then scroll through your choices in the Change Icon screen. After you've clicked on the one you want, choose OK to close the dialog box.

Starting Nuthin'

Poison: Empty Startup group

Some people have things in their Startup group. You've seen them. But yours is blank.

Antidote: The Startup group does what it says it will: starts programs automatically when you load Windows. Put programs you use daily in the Startup group (saves you a couple of point-and-clicks later).

To add programs to the Startup group, just drag the program icon from its current window to the Startup group. You can use that snazzy new Windows 3.1 drag-and-drop feature (which means you drag and drop the icon and it sticks. Amazing.). The next time you start Windows, your program will come to life before your eyes — no clicks needed.

Note: If you want to start the program but have it reduced to an icon, press Alt and double-click the icon and then click the Run Minimized check box.

52

S.O.S. For Windows

Come On and Join the Group

Poison: Missing program in the group

Your program doesn't show up anywhere in Windows's windows.

Antidote: Not all programs jump right into Windows and say "Here I am!" when they are installed. DOS programs are particularly shy. What you need to do is add that program (called a program item) to a group window.

Just open the group window and then choose New from the File menu. Select Program Item, click OK, add the program's

Program Manager Perils

name in the Description line, and, in the Command line, type the path and startup command you would use to start the command from the DOS prompt. It's that simple. (Enter the other stuff if you want, but it'll work with just the Command line.) Click OK, and there you have it.

Note: Hey, you don't have much time when killer bees are chasing you — but once you're out of danger, you can take some time to learn more about program items and groups by relaxing with Andy Rathbone's *Windows For Dummies* (IDG, 1992).

My Program Manager Doesn't Look Like That!

Poison: Manager impersonation

You thought you were using the same Windows everyone else had. But the window that comes up when you start Windows doesn't say Program

And other times, it's those darned earthquakes!

Manager. And it doesn't look like the Program Manager. And it doesn't quack like the Program Manager.

So you guess it's not the Program Manager.

Antidote: The Program Manager is Windows's answer to an organizer for the programs you start and work with. The Program Manager is not the only utility that does such a thing. There are others, called *shells*, from other manufacturers.

Windows makes it possible for you to use a different shell, if that's what you want, by including the SHELL= line in the [BOOT] section of SYSTEM.INI.

In this case, it sounds like someone else has installed another shell for you. To remove the shell= and return to Program Manager, just delete the filename after the equal sign.

Note: Whenever you're thinking about making changes to WIN.INI or SYSTEM.INI, make a backup copy of the file before you edit it. That way, if you want to return to your original, you've kept a copy.

C'Mon, Now, Share!

Poison: Network group problems

You want to add a new group window to your networked Windows, but you're having trouble.

Antidote: You can add a group to be shared by the network, but the group must be marked as read-only. To do that, set the attribute of the group to read-only; then place the file in a network directory that is shared. Others on your network can then use the group but not alter it; commands like Delete or Move will be disabled.

Program Manager Perils

Window Gigantus

Poison: One huge window

It's a bit disconcerting when you click on a button (accidentally on purpose, just to see what it does), and your window swells and swallows up everything else on-screen.

"I really did it this time," you think.

Antidote: Creating the large window is not as big a goof as you may think. It looks dramatic, yes, but it's not fatal. You just clicked on the Maximize button. Rather than seeing the Maximize button, you now should see a double-headed triangle. (What are they putting in the water these days?)

If you click on the double-headed triangle, the screen goes right back to the size it was BM (Before Maximize).

What's great about Maximize? The maximized window is big. You can't miss it. You'll recognize it once you've been there. You've got plenty of room to do stuff.

What's not great about Maximize? You can't see any other windows you've got open. You don't know what your other applications are up to. Your attention is held captive by this one program. You can't move between windows without some pretty clumsy movement.

Thin-Skinned Borders

Poison: Skinny borders

Being skinny isn't a real tragedy, unless you're a window border. And if you are a skinny window border, you're going to cause your user a whole lot of aggravation.

How to Make a Save-Your-Life Windows Disk

You could spend the next two minutes doing something really important. Like making that survival disk you've been putting off. Here's how.

Get into that File Manager, open the Disk menu, and choose Format Disk. Remember to make it a system disk. You know the ropes.

When the disk is formatted, use the Copy command (look in the File menu) to copy out the following files:

    AUTOEXEC.BAT
    CONFIG.SYS

You'll find those files in your root directory (C:\ or D:\). Now you need to go in and get the necessary INI files. First, change to the Windows directory and take a look at only your INI files by opening the View menu, choosing By File Type, and entering ***.INI** in the Name box. Now copy out the ones that look important (or all, if you're not sure). A few good candidates are any files ending in .INI or .GRP, including the following:

    WIN.INI
    SYSTEM.INI
    MOUSE.INI

Remember to label the disk clearly and put it somewhere safe and dry. And having a printout of those files easily accessible isn't a half-bad idea, either.

Where to Find a Good Witch Doctor

Even though you won't find a good witch doctor behind every palm tree, you can find one relatively easily:

- The technical support staff (the "help desk" or IS department) of your corporation

- The people who provide technical support by phone for the manufacturers of your hardware and software (there may be a fee)

- Trainers at computer training centers (some provide support after you take their classes)

- On-line computer-related forums (some are sponsored by software or hardware manufacturers)

- The experienced coworker in the next cubicle

- In the Yellow Pages, under Computer Consultants

- Knowledgeable salespeople at computer retail/service stores

- Members of your local computer society or user groups

- Your friends, your parents, your neighbors, and your kids!

If you're trying to resize the window by using the mouse, a great deal depends on being able to drag the border in the direction you want to resize. If the border is too narrow, you're going to have one heck of a time trying to drag it.

Antidote: You can change the border's thickness by getting into the Control Panel, double-clicking on Desktop, and increasing the Border Width settings in the Sizing Grid.

Missing Window

Poison: Program window lost

One of the most aggravating, but common, window woes is the missing window. You're messing around with a bunch of windows — leaving this program, starting that program — when a window disappears.

Antidote: The best way to find a lost window is not to look for it. Huh? Don't start frantically clicking on everything you can find. Who knows where you'll end up. Simply press Ctrl+Esc to bring everything back into balance (and put air back into your lungs).

Almost poetic, isn't it? Up pops a dialog box called the Task List — an unfriendly, DOS-ish looking box that has great power. Inside the dialog box are the applications you have running. Do you see the one you want? Good. Click on it so that it's highlighted and click on the Switch To button. There you are, with your window returned to the fold.

And all is right with the world.

You can figure out a a great deal about what's going on in Windows if you know which window is the active one. How do you tell when a window is active (besides looking for the mud on its tennis shoes, that is)?

An *active window* has a darkened (or colored) title bar (depending on whether you're using a monochrome or color monitor). Additionally, inside the active window, one of the program group icons (the currently selected icon) is highlighted.

Program Manager Perils

Don't look for the mouse pointer, because it can't tell you anything. The mouse, fickle thing, can roam about on the desktop and sit in any window, active or otherwise.

It's All How You Look at It

Poison: Window arrangement trouble

You're not real happy with this Task List thing. Sure, it helps when you've lost programs, but what about when you're looking for a specific group window inside the Program Manager?

Antidote: Windows gives you a whole variety of ways to display hidden windows:

- Press Alt+Esc to find a specific group window in the Program Manager.
- Press Alt+Tab to find an open program window.
- Press Ctrl+Esc to display the Task List.
- Open the Window menu and press the number of the open application you want.
- Choose the Cascade option to arrange windows so the title bar is visible for each window.
- Choose the Tile option to create a decoupage of open windows.

Off the Wall (paper) Windows

Poison: An almost out-of-reach window

Sometimes you get those renegade windows that try to sneak off when you're not looking. They gravitate farther and farther out until they are just a hair away from falling right off the edge of your screen.

But worst of all are the dreaded rock slides!

Antidote: If you can still click on a part of the window (any part that's visible will do), drag the window back inbounds. If you can't quite click on the window, press Alt+spacebar to display the Control menu. Then select Move. The pointer changes to a four-headed arrow, straight out of Star Trek. Use the arrow keys to move the window where you want it and press Enter. There you go, but you better give that window a good talking to.

Program Manager Perils

But I Closed the Window!

Poison: Memory errors with windows closed

You've been really conscientious about cleaning up after yourself. After you finish working with Excel, you neatly close up all the necessary windows. You didn't even leave any Program Manager window hanging about on-screen. And, still, when you try to load another program, you're getting an `Out of memory` error message.

Antidote: After you finish using a program, it may or may not free up the part of memory it was using. Don't assume that just because you've been neat and tidy, Windows has cleared out the area for new data.

Just to make sure that Windows isn't retaining little snippets of memory for no apparent reason, exit Windows once or twice a day if you change applications often. If you use the same program all day long, don't worry about it.

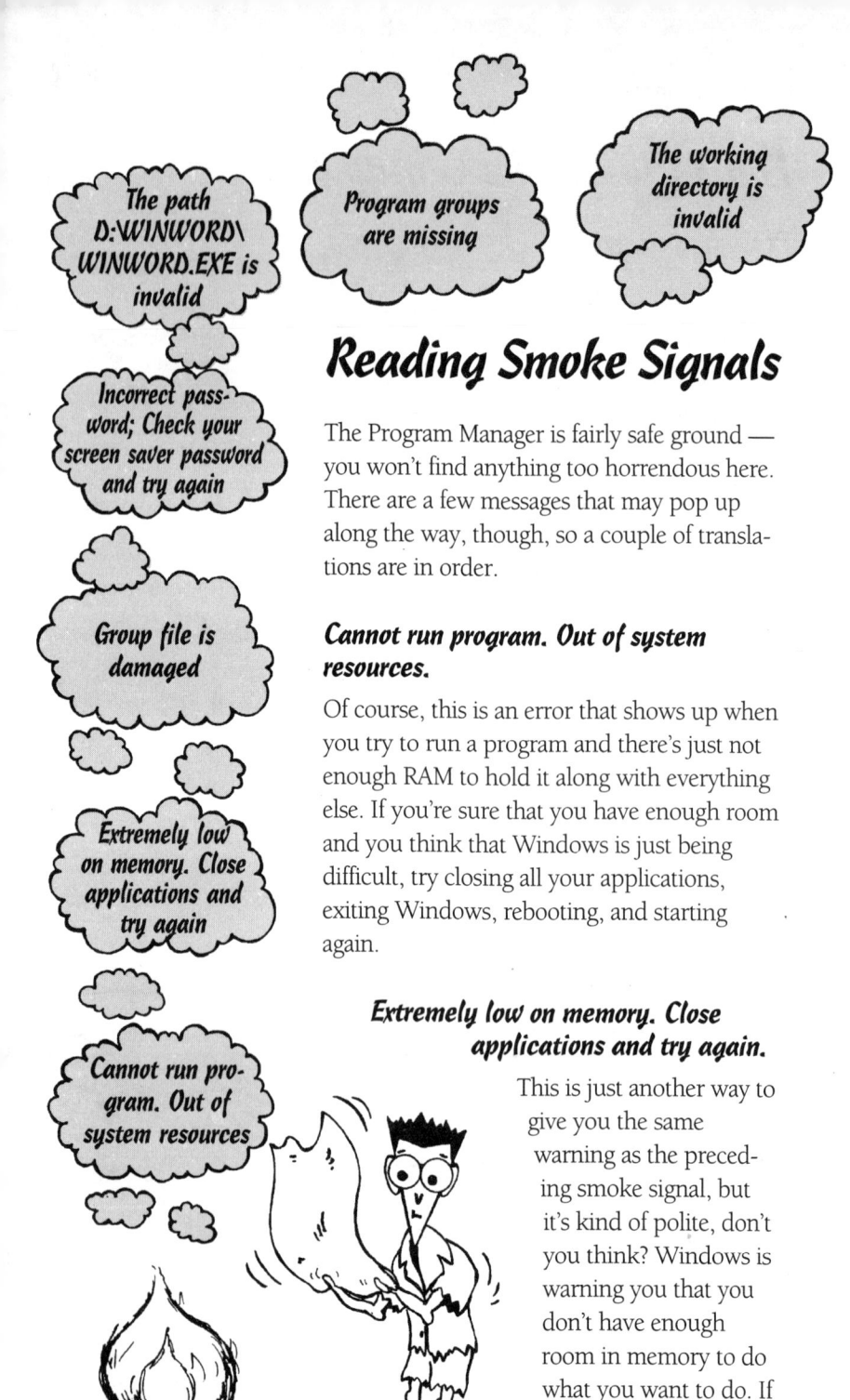

The path D:\WINWORD\WINWORD.EXE is invalid

Program groups are missing

The working directory is invalid

Incorrect password; Check your screen saver password and try again

Reading Smoke Signals

The Program Manager is fairly safe ground — you won't find anything too horrendous here. There are a few messages that may pop up along the way, though, so a couple of translations are in order.

Group file is damaged

Cannot run program. Out of system resources.

Of course, this is an error that shows up when you try to run a program and there's just not enough RAM to hold it along with everything else. If you're sure that you have enough room and you think that Windows is just being difficult, try closing all your applications, exiting Windows, rebooting, and starting again.

Extremely low on memory. Close applications and try again

Cannot run program. Out of system resources

Extremely low on memory. Close applications and try again.

This is just another way to give you the same warning as the preceding smoke signal, but it's kind of polite, don't you think? Windows is warning you that you don't have enough room in memory to do what you want to do. If you go ahead and try to

Program Manager Perils

run the program, you may have a crashing computer on your hands. If you're really stuck, get the witch doctor to show you some magic about freeing up more space in memory when you run Windows.

Group file is damaged

The one group you're trying to get to has something wrong with it. You can solve the problem with the SETUP /P command. And keep an eye on that group.

Incorrect password; Check your screen saver password and try again

Pressing Enter isn't going to do anything except get the same screen flashed back in your face. If you can't remember the password (you are using the right computer, aren't you?), you need to reboot and then turn off password protection in the Desktop's Screen Saver Setup.

The path D:\WINWORD\WINWORD.EXE is invalid

You may see such an error (not necessarily one for WINWORD.EXE) in a couple of different situations. You may have entered the wrong path in response to some prompt or another. You may have tried to start a program that isn't on your hard disk anymore. Or you may be looking for a file that has been corrupted. (Big sigh.) Use the File Manager to make sure that the programs are where they are supposed to be; then call the witch doctor if you get the same error again.

Program groups are missing

This is another message of the same PROGMAN.INI flavor. If one of your program groups gets corrupted or deleted, you may get this lukewarm warning (not that you wouldn't notice without it). Again, use SETUP /P to return everything to normal.

The working directory is invalid

You're trying to load a program (you just double-clicked on a program icon) and Windows is telling you that the directory it is looking for isn't there anymore. The program could have been moved or deleted, or something could be wrong with your hard disk. Use the File Manager to look for the directory in question and, if it's there as expected, have the witch doctor come over for a closer look.

Working with the windows on your Windows desktop is a relatively safe practice. Oh, sure, using Windows can drive you crazy when you lose things or delete programs you need. But in most cases, you don't get any seriously nasty errors by using Windows. Most of the errors you get have to do with used-up memory.

You Know You're Really in Trouble When...

Your computer keeps munching your PROGMAN.INI file

This is a good case for having a witch doctor looking over your shoulder. There's no good reason for a recurring case of disappearing groups, except perhaps a weird Setup or really strained memory. Windows can have a bad

> **Words of Wisdom: Dr. Watson**
>
> Dr. Watson is a Windows utility you can run in the background during your Windows session by typing **DRWATSON** in the Run dialog box. If you experience any GPFs (General Protection Faults), Dr. Watson records what was happening at the time of the error. Dr. Watson records findings in a file called DRWATSON.LOG, but you won't find the strange-looking notes much help — only the seriously technical can decipher the Dr.'s scratchings!

Program Manager Perils

group day, just like any of the rest of us, but when it continually munches your PROGMAN.INI file, it is probably possessed.

You install the same program in different groups

This is an easy thing to do. You set up a program to run in one group window, and then, three months later when you've all but forgotten you ever used the program to begin with, you put it somewhere else. The big problem with this double installation is that it eats up your storage space. Another problem is that you easily can have different versions of files in different directories.

You changed the names and icons of your program items just to be funny and now you can't remember what they were

This scenario is not very funny when you have to sit down to show an important department manager how you've done the layout of the corporate report. You suddenly wince when you remember that you've named PageMaker *SWAMPTHING*, with a little monster icon instead of the traditional one. The manager looks, one by one, at your icons. He decides you're having way too much fun.

Under the gun, you may not remember which program is which. But you can always press Alt and double-click on a program icon to show the properties of the icon. You can tell from the Command Line what the real name of the program is.

Chapter 3

File Manager Fiascoes

Paths through Peril

Sometimes it's the ho-hum things that are the most dangerous. Like washing your socks . . . in a piranha pool. The File Manager is supposed to take care of those boring disk, file, and directory duties for you. Not exciting stuff, certainly, but not as safe as you might think.

S.O.S. For Windows

File Manager Fiascoes

Weird... This all seems vaguely familiar, but different somehow. You know how you get that déja vu feeling sometimes? Or maybe it's more like a recurring bad dream....

All I've Got Is a Tree

Poison: No file display

Not everyone lucks into an ordinary File Manager the first time out. Chances are, someone's been playing with your Windows. Instead of seeing a directory tree and a file display like I promised you, you've got a rather bare-looking tree.

Antidote: Hey — that's the beauty of Windows. You've got an option for everything. Want to see more than that ugly tree? Open the View menu and choose Tree and Directory. Now the screen is split in two. See how easy that was?

Unreadable File Manager

Poison: Eye-strain fonts

If you installed Windows yourself, you probably see your average run-of-the-mill text when you open the File Manager. The font doesn't surprise you. But if someone else set things up for you, or if you've inherited someone else's machine, you may have a bit of an eye-opener when you display the File Manager for the first time. The File Manager lets you choose from a variety of fonts for your directory and file display. You can also choose whether you want everything shown in uppercase or lowercase letters.

Antidote: To find out how your File Manager is set and perhaps make a few changes, open the Options menu and choose Font. The font currently in use is shown in the Font: box. If you want to change the settings, try clicking on a couple of the fonts and watch the change in the Sample box. When you've got things the way you want them, click OK.

If the font looks okay to you, maybe you're having trouble reading the file names because they are too small. Try increasing the size or displaying the files in all caps (make sure there's no X in the Lowercase check box).

Note: For more information on formidable fonts, see Chapter 6.

Directory Windows Everywhere

Poison: Too much open

You've been so busy moving this file here and copying that file there that you didn't notice how crowded your display was getting. Where did all this stuff come from?

Antidote: If you move things around in a window, the File Manager opens a new window each time you click on a drive icon. Even if you've worked on drive C fourteen times before, the File Manager will continue to open windows if you move any of the files in the window you display. Pretty soon your File Manager area will be filled with cascading windows.

Make sure you close windows when you don't need them anymore. Not only do they confuse things, they eat up extra memory. To close them, just double-click on the control menu button in the upper left corner of the window.

You Formatted What?

Poison: Wrong-disk format

Boy, is this easy to do. Right after you click the OK button and mindlessly click Yes in the Confirm Format Disk dialog box, something in your brain goes

"Whaaa?"

and you, panic-stricken, realize that you've said "Sure, go ahead and format my work disk."

Antidote: If you originally formatted that disk using DOS 5.0 or later (or you were using Windows with DOS 5.0 or later), you'll be able to unformat the disk with a utility called UnFormat.

In order to use UnFormat, you'll have to exit to DOS. Because Windows leaves files open during operation, there's a chance that the files could be damaged or the UnFormat procedure could fail. Close Windows normally, and at the DOS prompt, type **UNFORMAT** and press Enter. Then follow the prompts.

The Invisible Disk

Poison: The File Manager doesn't see your disk.

There's the File Manager, waiting for you to do something. You put a disk in the drive and click on the A icon. Windows tells you that it's still waiting for a disk.

Antidote: Could be several things:

- Are you sure there's a disk in the drive?

- Is the disk inserted properly? Take the disk out and reinsert, just to make sure.

- Has the disk been formatted?

- If so, is the format for a capacity your drive can read?

- Can someone else's computer access the disk? (If not, it's the disk; if so, it's probably your disk drive.)

If you try all these things and nothing

helps, call the witch doctor. Cheer up, though. In most cases, the disk just isn't in the drive all the way.

File Manager's Not Listening

Poison: Can't see drive E

You recently added a CD-ROM, and you're still trying to figure out how to use it. You put the CD in the drive, open the File Manager, and click the drive E icon.

The File Manager says you need to insert the disk in drive E.

Antidote: Take a look at that CD. Chances are, it's either upside-down or the wrong sort of CD. You can display the contents of a CD only if it's a multimedia or reference CD — in other words, you're not going to get a list of Motown's Top Ten hits. No audio CDs for the File Manager. Leave that for the Music Box.

Note: For more about using multimedia stuff — such as CD-ROMs and sound boards — with Windows, see Chapter 8.

That's Not What's on My Disk!

Poison: Erroneous file display

You glance at the file list on the right side of the File Manager. Then you look closer. Those aren't the files on this disk. At least, those aren't *supposed* to be the files on this disk.

Antidote: No need to panic. You didn't overwrite the disk you needed. The File Manager just took a little break. To tell File Manager to take a look at the disk, open the Window menu and choose Refresh. Now you see those important files. If you choose Refresh and File Manager doesn't show you the files on your disk, you've got a potential hardware problem. Better get the witch doctor in on this one.

All My Graphics Files Are Gone!

Poison: Temporarily missing files

You're getting the hang of this File Manager thing. Looked a little frightening at first, but the concept is simple enough. Find the directory you want to see, point, and click.

When you change to your PAINTBRUSH directory, however, all those beautiful bitmaps you've been working on have vanished.

After you stop hyperventilating, you'll be able to see what *really* happened. (Who knows? The extra oxygen might help.)

File Manager Fiascoes

Antidote: You can set the File Manager to display whatever files you want. You can display DOC files (that is, files that end in DOC, like Word files), EXE files, BAT files, BMP files, GIF files, and on and on and on.

If the File Manager is set to display all files, the following is displayed at the top of the window:

```
C:\*.*
```

(Yours may or may not show C:\. The *.* is the important part.) If your File Manager is set to show only DOC files, the line will look like this:

```
C:\*.DOC
```

That means that only files ending with DOC appear in the file list on the right side of the screen. You can change that (so that you can see your bitmap — BMP — files) by opening the View menu and selecting the By File Type option. Enter *.* in the Name box and click OK. Now the File Manager should show all the files (even those you don't want to see.)

Disk Copy Flops

Poison: A stalled copy

Copying a disk is one of the safest computer tasks you'll do on a regular basis. You're not deleting anything; you're not formatting anything. Just putting a copy of the contents of this disk onto that disk.

Simple enough.

Antidote: If the File Manager runs into a problem, it will display a message alerting you that the copy operation is going sour. If your copy goes bad, check the following things:

- Is there a disk in the drive you're copying from?
- Is there a disk in the drive you're copying to?
- Are the disks inserted correctly?

🡆 Are both disks the same capacity?

🡆 Is the receiving disk write-protected? (It shouldn't be.)

When you're working with DOS, it's important that a disk be formatted before you try copying information to it. Not so in Windows. When you're copying a disk, Windows will format the receiving disk for you before the data is copied over.

Sorry, No Association

Poison: File has no associated application.

Other people in your office are able to start Microsoft Word for Windows by simply clicking on a DOC file in their WINWORD directory.

File Manager Fiascoes

When you click a .DOC file, you get a message like

```
Cannot find file (or one of its components).
```

or

```
No association exists
```

Antidote: File Manager does let you click on a data file and move right to the program that uses it. But first you need to associate the file (see Techie Term sidebar for a definition of *associate*).

To associate the file, select the one you want and choose Associate from the File menu. Choose the program from the Associate With: list and then click OK.

Note: If the program you want to associate with the file isn't shown in the Associate With: box, click on Browse to move through other disks or directories on your system.

Directory in Hiding

Poison: A missing directory

You're getting ready to copy a few files out to disk for a coworker. (We won't tell anyone it's Tetris.) But all of a sudden you realize — with horror — that the TETRIS directory is missing.

Antidote: There could be a couple of reasons for this:

Techie Term

When you *associate* a file type with a particular program, you are linking an application (like Excel) with a file extension (like .XLS). After the file type is associated, you can go right into the program and open a file by simply double-clicking the filename.

- You deleted the directory and forgotaboutit(notlikely).

- Someone else got on your machine and deleted it (*really* not likely).

- You've collapsed the display of your directories, and since you buried TETRIS way back where your boss wouldn't see it, it's hidden (possible).

- It's really in there, but you just missed it as you were reading through (very possible).

If it's there, you'll find it with the Search command (in the File menu). In the Search For: box, type the directory you're looking for (if you can't remember the exact spelling, use a wildcard character, like SOL*.*). In the Start From: box, enter where you want to begin looking. If you want Windows to look everywhere, leave Search All Subdirectories checked. When you click OK, the File Manager starts searching.

The Search Results window shows you the places where the File Manager has found the characters you entered. You can start a program directly from this screen or copy, move, rename, or delete files; however, you can't change to another directory in the Search Results window. For that, go back to the File Manager.

Note: This Search bit works for files, too. Just type the name of the file you're looking for — or part of the file name and any necessary wildcard characters — in the Search For: box.

A File-Selection Nightmare

Poison: Trouble selecting files

What could be easier? You want to copy a file, so you point the mouse and click. There. File selected. Now open the File menu and choose Copy. Isn't File Manager fun?

File Manager Fiascoes

But what about those times when you want this file but not that one, and then this one over here, and that one in that column ... and you don't want to repeat the copy procedure 15 different times? Wouldn't it be nice to select just the files you need — even if they aren't right next to each other — and copy the ones you want?

Antidote: To select files in a row, press Shift while you click. Want files that aren't next to each other? Press Ctrl and click. How about all the files in the directory? Ctrl and /.

Let My Files Go!

Poison: Forever-selected files

Now you've highlighted every file in the directory and when you press Esc to remove the highlighting, nothing happens. A wave of panic rushes through you. You mean you'll have to *do* something with all those files you selected?

Antidote: You can deselect files a couple of different ways:

- *The easy way:* Click a different directory. Look. All gone.

- *The next easiest way:* Press Ctrl and \.

- *The way you'll never use:* Open the File menu and choose Select Files. Then click Deselect.

Scrambled Files and Toast

Poison: A badly garbled file

You're finally ready to work on that report you started last week and have been putting off as long as possible. Now it's do or die.

You open the file and see, well, *parts* of the report. But there's also part of that letter to your brother and your take-these-things-on-vacation list. Oh, no. There's even part of your Things-I'll-Ask-For-At-Review list. Sure hope nobody else has seen that.

Antidote: The best antidote really isn't one. If you've kept a backup of all your important files, having one bite the dust is no big deal. Just copy the necessary report file off your backup and you're back in business.

Why do files get scrambled? Most don't. But when they do, trying to unscramble them will eventually send you screeching down the hall. A file could get scrambled because:

- There's a bad spot on the disk where the file was written.

- Something interfered with the way the file was saved (the computer was moved or the disk drive door was opened during the operation).

- It's a seriously used disk that's giving out.

- You kept the disk close to something magnetized (like that paper clip holder or your coworker's personality).

Am I Moving or Copying?

Poison: Move-copy confusion

At first, it's kind of funny to watch. When you click on that filename and start to drag it out of the file list, will you be copying or moving? Sometimes you don't know until a message appears on your screen saying

```
Are you sure you want to move the selected files to D:\NORTON?
```

Oh, you've *moving* a file.

Next time you pull a file out, the message is

```
Are you sure you want to copy the selected files to C:\?
```

Now you're *copying*?

Antidote: The File Manager wants to make your life easier. For that reason, you can just drag a file when you want to move or copy it. The drag-and-drop feature is new with Windows 3.1.

But this trick is a little quirky. Dragging a file — when you're dragging it from one place on a disk to another place on the same disk — *moves* the file. But dragging a file from one disk to another winds up *copying* the file.

Head spinning? Here's a simple way around it:

- When you want to move a file, press Alt and drag the file.
- When you want to copy the file, press Ctrl and drag the file.

How to Make Backups

No kidding — a backup is the surest path back to functioning files. If you accidentally delete a subdirectory and don't realize it for a week and a half, those files will be gone forever. But if you have a backup (and even better, if you make backups regularly), you can restore the files you accidentally fried.

You can choose several methods to back up your files. You can copy out to disk important files, but that is a short-term fix. If your hard disk ever crashes, you're going to need all the programs and data. You can use a backup utility (there are several good ones out there) that will go in and back everything up. You can use the DOS command BACKUP — either from DOS or from the Tools menu in Windows, if you're using DOS 6.0 or later.

If you're using the basic DOS BACKUP command, have plenty of formatted disks handy. Then put the first disk in the drive, type **BACKUP**, and follow the prompts.

Also, if you're hooked up to a network, don't attempt to do your own backing up until you talk to the network administrator or someone on your technical support staff. You never know what evils lurk inside those network tentacles.

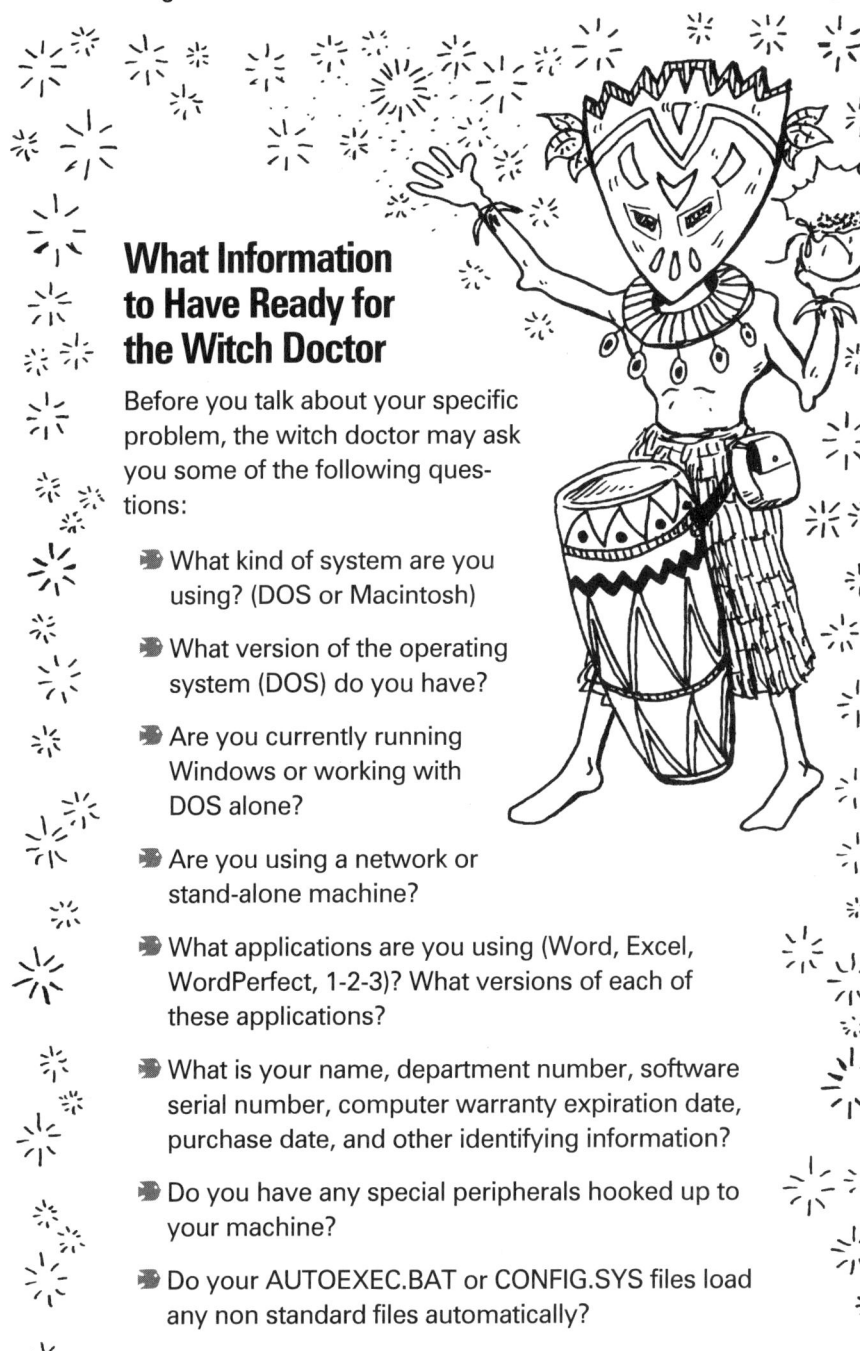

What Information to Have Ready for the Witch Doctor

Before you talk about your specific problem, the witch doctor may ask you some of the following questions:

- What kind of system are you using? (DOS or Macintosh)
- What version of the operating system (DOS) do you have?
- Are you currently running Windows or working with DOS alone?
- Are you using a network or stand-alone machine?
- What applications are you using (Word, Excel, WordPerfect, 1-2-3)? What versions of each of these applications?
- What is your name, department number, software serial number, computer warranty expiration date, purchase date, and other identifying information?
- Do you have any special peripherals hooked up to your machine?
- Do your AUTOEXEC.BAT or CONFIG.SYS files load any non standard files automatically?

Delete Terrors

Poison: Deleted files you really need

Yes, welcome to the world of tried-and-true computer users. Blowing away a really necessary file is one of the first rites of passage for new computerists.

Antidote: The best remedy is to have a backup right at your fingertips. You can just grab the necessary disks and have that file back on your computer in no time.

Oh. No backup? Well, you're in luck. The delete spirits aren't feeling too malevolent today. Here's a special trick they've agreed to let you in on:

1. Open the File menu and choose Run.

2. Type **C:\DOS\UNDELETE** (or if DOS is on D, use D:\ instead).

3. Click OK.

   Windows bumps you out to DOS, which runs the Undelete utility. Your file appears something like this:

   ```
   ?ILE    DOC    1345    12-23-93    11:57a    Undelete (Y/N)?
   ```

File Manager Fiascoes

Words of Wisdom: UNDELETE

UNDELETE is a DOS utility that runs back out to the disk and says "Hey, wait — I needed that!" to your files allocation table. If you recognize soon — like right away — that you've blown away a file you really need, you can run the UNDELETE command (open the File menu, choose Run, and type **UNDELETE**) to recover it.

DOS 6 Note: If you can't remember the exact name of the file you deleted and don't want to look through a gazillion files one at a time, enter **UNDELETE/LIST**. You'll see a listing of all the recently demised files waiting for you to bring them back to life.

4. Press Y; then, when prompted, press the first character in the filename to replace ?. You are then returned to the File Manager.

5. What? The file's not there? Open the Window menu and choose Refresh. The screen is updated and your file should appear.

Good news and bad news on Undelete: The good news is that if you don't remember the first character of the filename, you can type any character and DOS will still rescue the file. The bad news is that if you're using a version of DOS pre-5.0, you're out of luck on an undelete feature, unless you've got another program — like Quick Unerase — that can do it for you.

Reading Smoke Signals

A quiet sort, the File Manager isn't in the habit of displaying beaucoup error messages. And generally the ones you receive aren't too frightening. Although, you might see a few of the following:

No matching files were found

Cannot replace FILENAME: Access Denied

Cannot rename FILENAME: Cannot find file

Cannot format disk

Cannot format disk

Well, Windows doesn't like that disk. Check to make sure that it's not write-protected or damaged in any way. You may want to exit to DOS and try using the FORMAT command if you suspect that the disk may be corrupted. Another problem that can cause this error is using the wrong density disk in the wrong density drive.

Cannot rename FILENAME: Cannot find file

Here you're trying to rename a file that Windows can't find. In most cases, when you use Rename, you're going to click on the file, and then open the File menu and choose the Rename command. This enters the name of the file you want to rename in the From: box automatically. If you decide you'd like to rename another file, however, and type one in yourself, you might get this message. Make sure you've typed the name right (and that you've specified the correct path, if it's in a directory other than the current one); and then try again.

File Manager Fiascoes

Cannot replace FILENAME: Access Denied

You're trying to copy a file out to disk. The disk already has a file with the same name on it. That's okay, you say. No it's not, says Windows. Check to make sure the disk still has room on it (use the File Manager to find out). You can also determine whether the file is write-protected by clicking on the file, opening the File menu, and choosing Properties. A write-protected file will have the Read Only box checked.

No matching files were found

You were using Search (from the File menu) to find a file or directory and you entered something Windows couldn't find. Did you use a wildcard character? Check your spelling (and the place you started the search) and try again.

You Know You're Really in Trouble When...

Remember that a recent backup of your files and programs is the surest way out of "I-lost-my-files!" panic. You may have DOS 5.0 or a witch doctor with some pretty good magic, but keeping a current backup is the best preventative medicine there is.

You format a disk you need, and you don't have DOS 5.0 or later

This isn't good. DOS 5.0 brings with it an UnFormat utility that can save most of the data from a recently formatted disk. Data protection is a beautiful thing. Call your witch doctor as soon as possible and don't mess with anything else on your computer until he gets there. If you open and close files — or even Windows — the space your files occupied may be updated and overwritten with new information. Let the witch doctor attempt some of that magic he does so well.

You move files off your hard disk to a floppy and then lose the floppy

Ha — this is possible (I've done it). "Oh, I'll label it in a minute," I said, as I reached around my printer to answer the phone. Two weeks later, I found the disk shuffled inside the back cover of a notebook I'd been using. In the meantime, Chapters 4, 5, and 6 had been missing.

You delete an entire directory, don't have enough memory to run Undelete, and don't have a backup

This is one of those only-on-Friday-the-13th-when-the-moon-is-full kinds of errors, but it could happen. The moral? Back up your data! (And keep it somewhere safe but close enough that you can get to it when you need it.)

Chapter 4

Wicked Windows Applications

Paths through Peril

Well, at least you're in familiar territory: Windows programs in Windows. Things should go smoothly now. But then the ground starts shifting beneath your feet and you find yourself face to face with things you've never seen before. Wouldn't it be nice to have a day without surprises?

The Bad Install

Poison: Install litter

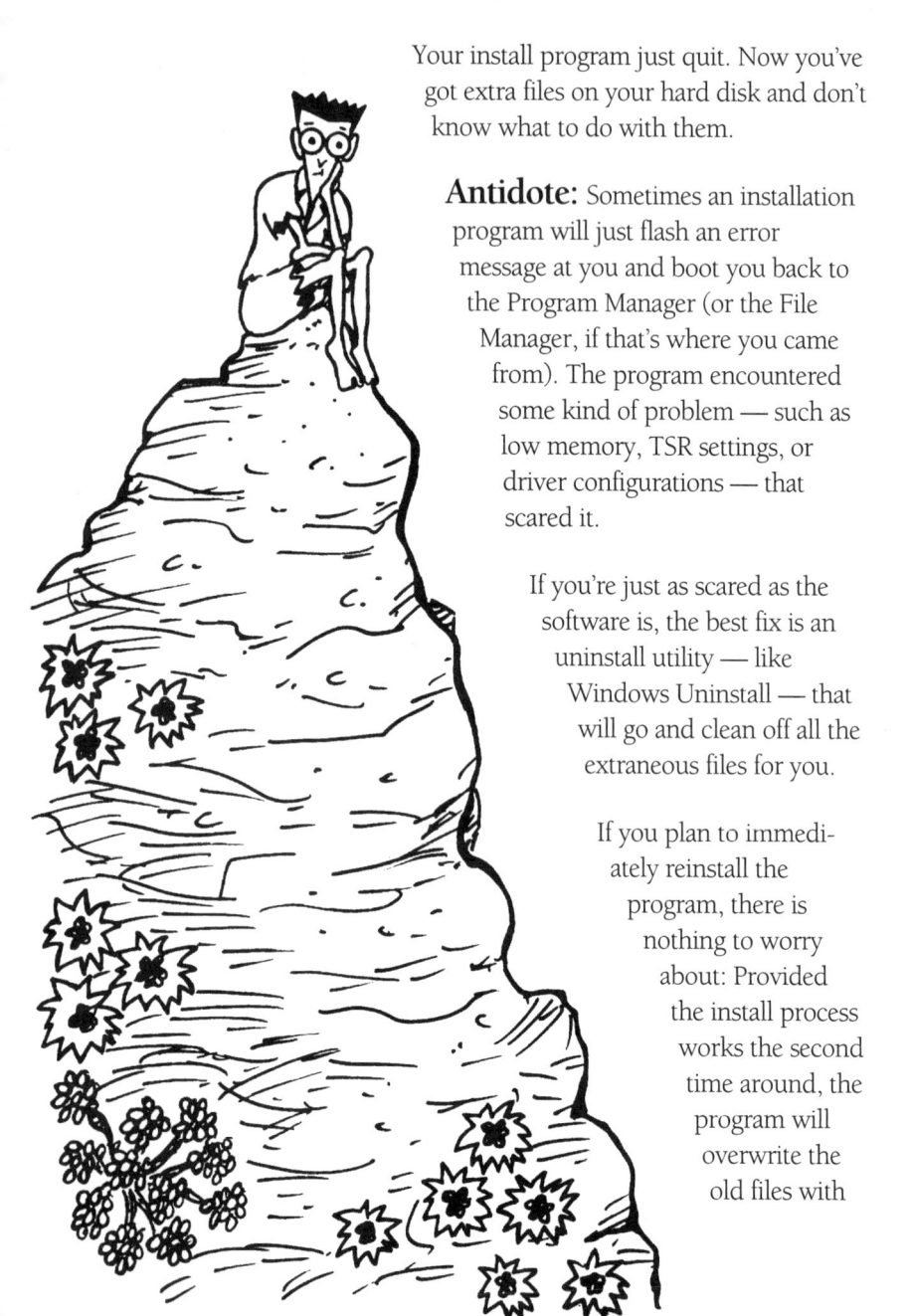

Your install program just quit. Now you've got extra files on your hard disk and don't know what to do with them.

Antidote: Sometimes an installation program will just flash an error message at you and boot you back to the Program Manager (or the File Manager, if that's where you came from). The program encountered some kind of problem — such as low memory, TSR settings, or driver configurations — that scared it.

If you're just as scared as the software is, the best fix is an uninstall utility — like Windows Uninstall — that will go and clean off all the extraneous files for you.

If you plan to immediately reinstall the program, there is nothing to worry about: Provided the install process works the second time around, the program will overwrite the old files with

Wicked Windows Applications

the new ones of the same name and if the program works right, there's no harm done.

If you won't be able to install the program because of the error and want to clean those extra files off your hard disk, be very very careful. Don't remove anything you're not absolutely sure about.

Best advice for deleting files? When in doubt, *don't*.

Words of Wisdom: Windows Uninstall

One of the tricky things about working with Windows applications is that when Windows installs a program, it may spread files out in various directories of your hard disk. That means that getting rid of the program isn't a simple matter of going right to that directory and deleting it. There may be INI files in one directory, DRV files in another, and who-knows-what files somewhere else.

One popular third-party utility that finds all the pieces of a program and removes them is Windows Uninstall. If you don't have a copy of a utility that will uninstall the program for you, check your program's documentation for instructions on how to remove it. If the manual doesn't tell you how, call the manufacturer. Many of the program files used in Windows look similar and one innocent click of the mouse button could result in your blowing away a file that cripples another program.

How to Make a System Configuration Backup

Backing up your programs and data is important, but it's also important to record the way your system is set up. These special settings about your system are known as the system configuration.

You can use MSD to get a quick look of at your computer's important stuff. MSD is really a DOS tool, but you can also run it within Windows (although you will see a note from Microsoft that things might be a bit more accurate if you run MSD from *outside* Windows). MSD displays the information to the screen, but you can have MSD dump all the info in a file for you by typing

MSD /F C:\INFO.MSD

and pressing Enter. MSD does a quick survey and puts the file INFO.MSD on your root directory. It's a good idea to store INFO.MSD on that Windows survival disk so it's ready for the witch doctor when the need arises.

And won't he be impressed?

If you are having problems with you computer that you think may not be due specifically to Windows, remember to consult *S.O.S. For DOS, DOS For Dummies,* and *Upgrading and Fixing PCs For Dummies* (all from IDG) for additional information.

What Stuff to Have Ready for the Witch Doctor

When the witch doctor arrives and sees that you have the contents of your satchel all ready for him, he will be pleased. He might even get your problem fixed faster. Looks like carrying all this stuff around is finally going to pay off:

- A written (or printed) copy of any error messages you've gotten
- Printouts of CONFIG.SYS and AUTOEXEC.BAT
- Notes you made about the problem
- MSD printout from your system
- Your Dr. Watson information
- Your most recent backup
- Your program disks (originals and/or working copies)
- The manuals for your hardware and software
- Any other books you have related to your system or software
- Munchies (always appreciated)

The Big Lock Up

Poison: Stalled program

Learning new software is scary enough without some big bad program stopping in the middle. Programus interruptus.

Antidote: How a program reacts when lockup occurs depends on the program. You might see an error message. Your computer might just freeze. First, write down any errors you see. Then ask yourself these things:

- **Is the installation disk inserted correctly?** (Remove it and reinsert it, just to be sure.)

- **Are you sure you've got a total lockup?** Try pressing Esc to see whether you've got a total lockup or something smaller (and smellier), like a dead mouse. If you're totally locked up, reboot (that's Ctrl+Alt+Del).

- **Could RAM be a problem?** On your way back in to Windows, check your available memory. (You can use the DOS MEM command or the About the Program Manager, in the Windows Help menu.)

- **Is SMARTDRV.EXE included in your AUTOEXEC.BAT file?**

🕷 **Do you have enough disk storage for the program?** The File Manager will tell you that.

If your computer is totally locked up, reboot. Then start Dr. Watson (the utility that runs behind the scenes and records any error messages) by opening the File menu, choosing Run, and typing **DRWATSON**. Then restart your program. If you get a GPF (General Protection Fault) when you try to run the program again, Dr. Watson will have recorded the particulars.

Finding Fault for Multiple Lockups

Poison: Program or Windows?

You've been experiencing repeated lockups with this program. Because the program runs in Windows, it's hard to tell whether there's something wrong with Windows, the program, or your system.

Antidote: Ask yourself these questions:

🕷 Were you working with the same program when previous lockups occurred?

🕷 Were you performing the same operation (sorting, spelling, linking, merging, etc.)?

🕷 Did you have the same data file open when the previous problems occurred?

If you answer Yes to any (or all) of these questions, you may have a problem with the program you are running in Windows. It could be a single file that's corrupted (although you would be likely to get an error message — not a lockup — with a damaged file). More likely, there's a conflict in settings Windows and the program share.

If the lockups seem random to you, make a list of what program you were using and what operation you were performing when each of the lockups happened. Keep the list beside your computer so you can add any new lockups to the list. If the lockups continue, consult your witch doctor and hand over your accumulated documentation.

GPF Doesn't Mean Go Play Football

Poison: General Protection Fault

Getting a General Protection Fault error isn't pleasant. But it's better than getting a UAE (Unrecoverable Application Error), which is what a similar situation would present in Windows 3.0. In 3.0, when you got a UAE, your system totally locked up and you had to reboot to get out of the freeze. With a GPF, you should still exit Windows and start again.

Words of Wisdom: Windows SmartDrive

SmartDrive is a disk caching utility that helps Windows work a little faster. SmartDrive is included with Windows (and was updated in DOS 6.2) and should be loaded automatically at startup by your AUTOEXEC.BAT file. The line that should be in there (add it if it isn't) is one of the following:

```
C:\WINDOWS\SMARTDRV.EXE
C:\DOS\SMARTDRV.EXE
```

If your copy of Windows is on D or is in a different directory, substitute the right drive and directory for your particular system. SmartDrive allows Windows to create a special reserved portion of RAM for data it can swap in and out, thus speeding up the time Windows takes to read and write to disk.

So consider yourself lucky.

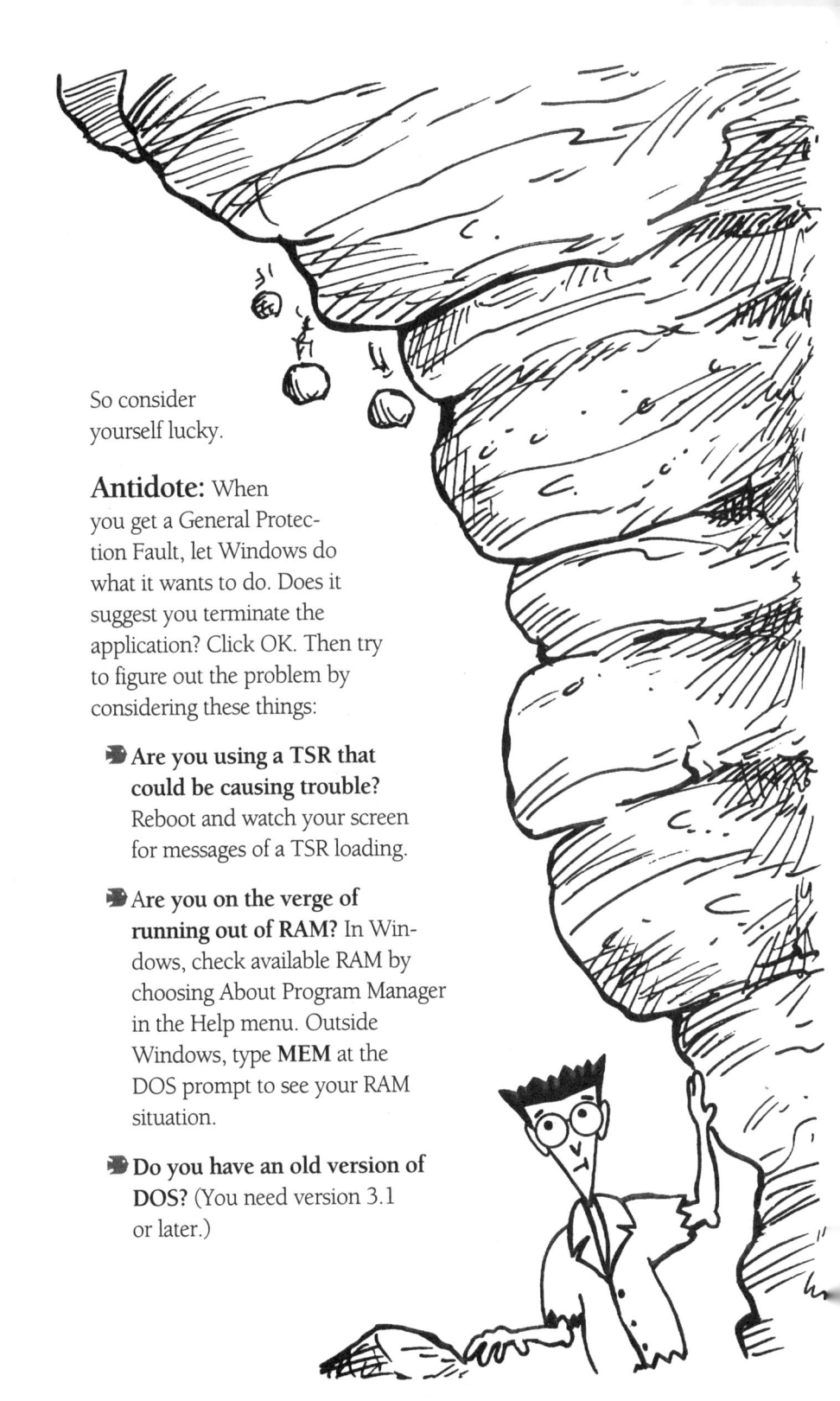

Antidote: When you get a General Protection Fault, let Windows do what it wants to do. Does it suggest you terminate the application? Click OK. Then try to figure out the problem by considering these things:

- **Are you using a TSR that could be causing trouble?** Reboot and watch your screen for messages of a TSR loading.

- **Are you on the verge of running out of RAM?** In Windows, check available RAM by choosing About Program Manager in the Help menu. Outside Windows, type **MEM** at the DOS prompt to see your RAM situation.

- **Do you have an old version of DOS?** (You need version 3.1 or later.)

- Is Windows set up to correctly run with your hardware? (Use Setup to make sure.)

- Have you had a problem with this application before? (It could be the program itself.)

- Does the application load into high memory? There could be a possible memory conflict.

Before you start the application again, turn on Dr. Watson (type **DRWATSON** in the Run dialog box and click OK). He'll keep a record of what's going on so that, if your application crashes again, you'll have documentation for the witch doctor.

Techie Term

The *GPF* — General Protection Fault — is a special error message Windows 3.1 reserves for Big Stuff.

Afraid of Germs?

Poison: Virus dread

A couple times a year, word circulates about a Big Virus that's going to knock everyone's computer out. From the White House to Ma Bell to the corner grocery. Last year, it was Michelangelo. Next year it will be something else. You're afraid to use any files from anywhere — unless they're shrinkwrapped.

Antidote: There are many things you can do to protect your programs and data from viruses:

- Use an anti-virus utility to check for possible viruses on your disk (DOS 6.0 has AntiVirus, a utility that loads right into the Tools menu in the Program Manager).

- Only accept programs (and, specifically, disks) from people you know.
- Download files only from established on-line services.
- Check every file you add to your computer from another source for a possible infection.

The anti-virus utilities are simple to use, relatively inexpensive, and can save you a priceless amount of work and worry. VSAFE and MSAV come with DOS 6.2 and can load directly into Windows.

The Data Linking Game

Poison: OLE, DDE, or Paste?

Sometimes it's hard to know — when you've got several options — which one is the one you need. When you are trying to paste an Excel chart into your Word for Windows document, how do you know whether you have to figure out OLE, DDE, or just plain Paste?

Antidote: First, think about what you're trying to accomplish. All three of these methods get the chart into the document. But here's the difference:

- Paste just pastes it there.
- DDE pastes it there and updates it when you change the Excel chart in Excel.
- OLE pastes it, changes it when you modify the chart, and lets you move directly into Excel when you double-click the chart.

When there's a question, choose OLE over DDE. You'll know when you need Paste. But OLE gives you more punch — and more options. Being able to move right to the application that generated the information can be a great benefit, especially when you're trying to get a report done under the wire and you can't quite get the spreadsheet to balance.

Is OLE a Lot of Bull?

Poison: No-link OLE

You tried copying a piece of art from Designer into Word for Windows, just to try out this way-cool OLE thing. You double-clicked the picture. Nothing happened.

Antidote: Even though the concept of OLE seems pretty advanced, there are relatively few things that can go wrong:

- Do both applications support OLE?
- Are you sure you inserted and copied the object? (Do it again, just to make sure.)
- Did you select Insert Object? (Is it an option? If not, your application might not support OLE.)
- Are the files OLECLI.DLL and OLESVR.DLL in your C:\WINDOWS\SYSTEM directory? Use File Manager to check.

If the answer to all these is Yes, you should be able to embed the object. Try a small experiment — like inserting a small piece of art from Paintbrush into Write. Once you get the basics figured out, you can tackle the higher-end jobs.

Techie Term

OLE is an acronym for Object Linking and Embedding, a Windows feature that lets your programs share data easily. You can create a spreadsheet in one document, for example, and then insert the spreadsheet in a word processing program. The link allows you to double-click the imported spreadsheet and move right to the spreadsheet program from within your word processor. See? Even the hard stuff is getting easier.

This really shouldn't be a problem. The trick is all in the concentration. And if you come prepared, it's really a piece of cake...

Note: One of the greatest things about OLE is that you can embed other objects right in your files. Leave a wake-up call for someone reading a boring document. Put an icon in there that takes the reader right to Solitaire. (You could put an object in that would take a reader to more work, but who wants to do *that?*)

The DDE Connection

Poison: Alarming DDE messages

You were ready to close the file, and Windows shocks you with a dramatic message about severing the connection between the embedded object and the receiving application. Are you about to ruin your OLE object forever? Should you continue?

Antidote: What this message is saying is that by saving and closing the object that is linked to the other document, you are closing the information channel between them. Windows wants to know if you want to update the link before closing. Click Yes.

Later, when you reopen the document with the embedded document, Windows will know if you've changed the item in the source document. If there's been a change, Windows says

```
This document contains links to other
documents. Do you want to update links now?
```

Click Yes to get the most current version of the embedded document updated in your file.

Multiple DDE Injuries

Poison: Two many DDEs

As you know, it's easy to get into window overload in Windows. You open this window — go and check something over there — come back and change this window — and before you know it, you've got 13 open files on the screen. When you are trying to use OLE, having more than one open copy of the same file can get really confusing.

Antidote: Make sure that you've selected and copied the most current version of the data to the linked document. Then minimize the documents you are using and, one by one, inspect and close the unnecessary files. Unexpected links aren't much fun — especially when you're trying to finish a report and get out of Dodge before sundown.

Really — it's no sweat. . . .

Where's DDE When You Need It?

Poison: Lost DDE links

You're trying to use DDE to link data from one file to another, and the link isn't working.

Antidote: Are you sure you've linked the data correctly? Open the file and highlight the item you want to link. Choose Copy. Go to the receiving document and open the Edit menu. Choose Paste Link. The item is placed at the cursor position. The link is established.

If you don't have a Paste Link command in your Edit menu, the application doesn't support DDE. (Not all applications do.)

Open the file you want to link, select data, choose Copy. Go to the receiving application, choose Paste Link.

That's a hot link.

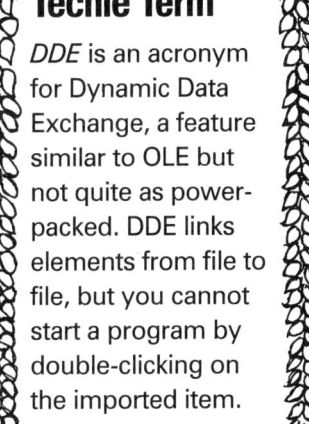

> **Techie Term**
>
> *DDE* is an acronym for Dynamic Data Exchange, a feature similar to OLE but not quite as power-packed. DDE links elements from file to file, but you cannot start a program by double-clicking on the imported item.

Too Much Updating Going On

Poison: DDE is updating too often

DDE updates every time I turn around. Once in a while would be fine.

Antidote: You can control how often DDE updates the changes in the source document by changing the link from Automatic to Manual. Open the Edit menu and choose Links. Then click Manual; then click OK. Some applications update links when you press F9. To determine what keystroke updates the links in your program, consult your program's manual.

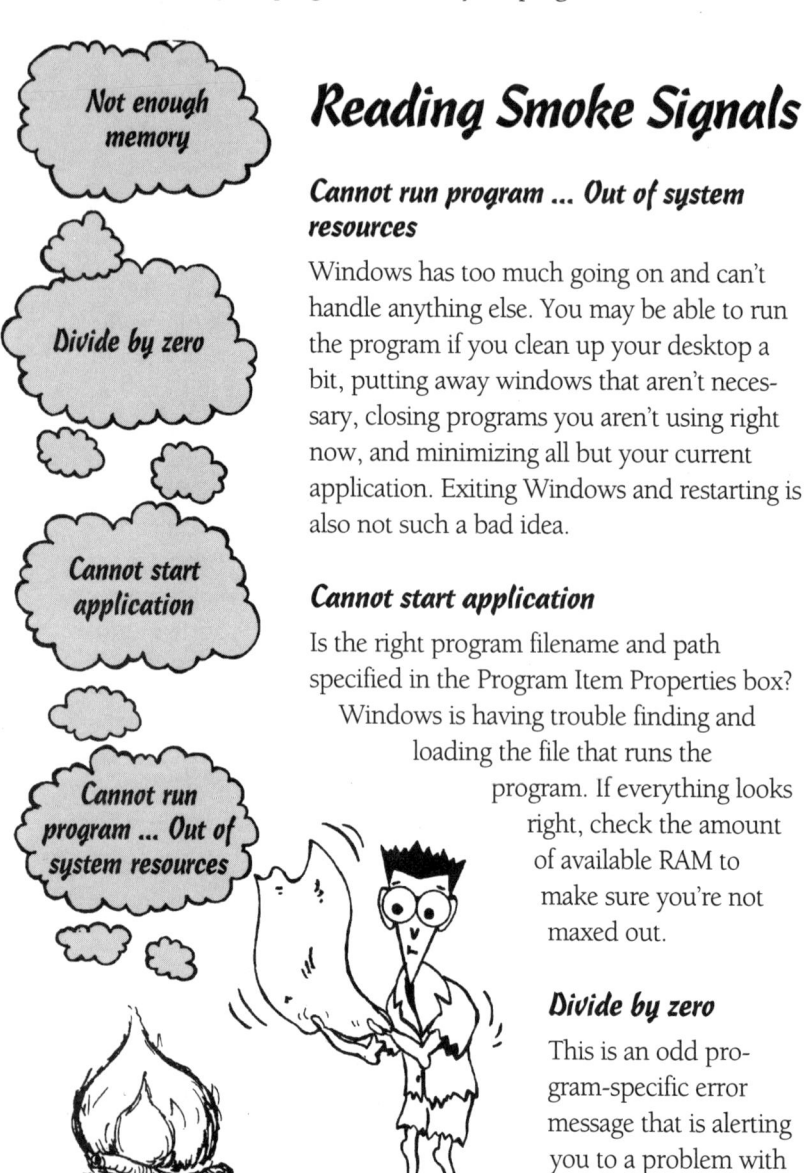

Not enough memory

Divide by zero

Cannot start application

Cannot run program ... Out of system resources

Reading Smoke Signals

Cannot run program ... Out of system resources

Windows has too much going on and can't handle anything else. You may be able to run the program if you clean up your desktop a bit, putting away windows that aren't necessary, closing programs you aren't using right now, and minimizing all but your current application. Exiting Windows and restarting is also not such a bad idea.

Cannot start application

Is the right program filename and path specified in the Program Item Properties box? Windows is having trouble finding and loading the file that runs the program. If everything looks right, check the amount of available RAM to make sure you're not maxed out.

Divide by zero

This is an odd program-specific error message that is alerting you to a problem with your application, not with Windows. In most cases, rebooting will put things straight.

Not enough memory

There's no doubt about this error, is there? Again, a RAM issue. Free up everything you can, and if that still isn't enough, call the witch doctor.

You Know You're Really in Trouble When...

Every time you run a certain program, Windows hangs up

You've probably got a corrupted program file. If you're comfortable doing so, you can try reinstalling the program. If that doesn't help, call technical support (or ask someone close who's familiar with the program) and find out if there are any software updates you should be aware of. At the least, you can explain the error you're receiving and request a replacement file.

Your computer made a noise like a crashing airplane, and now it won't boot

Get out your boot disk and take a look at the mess the virus made of your startup files. Some viruses are more bark than bite; they cause panic among their victims but relatively little damage to files. Don't go toying around with your system after a suspected virus-caused crash; go straight to the witch doctor and let him bring the necessary medicinal herbs.

Part II

Where Do I Go Now?

Oooohhh Nooooo! Here we go again. This is definitely serious bad news. You get that awful feeling in the pit of your stomach again, and you just know that there's no easy way out this time.

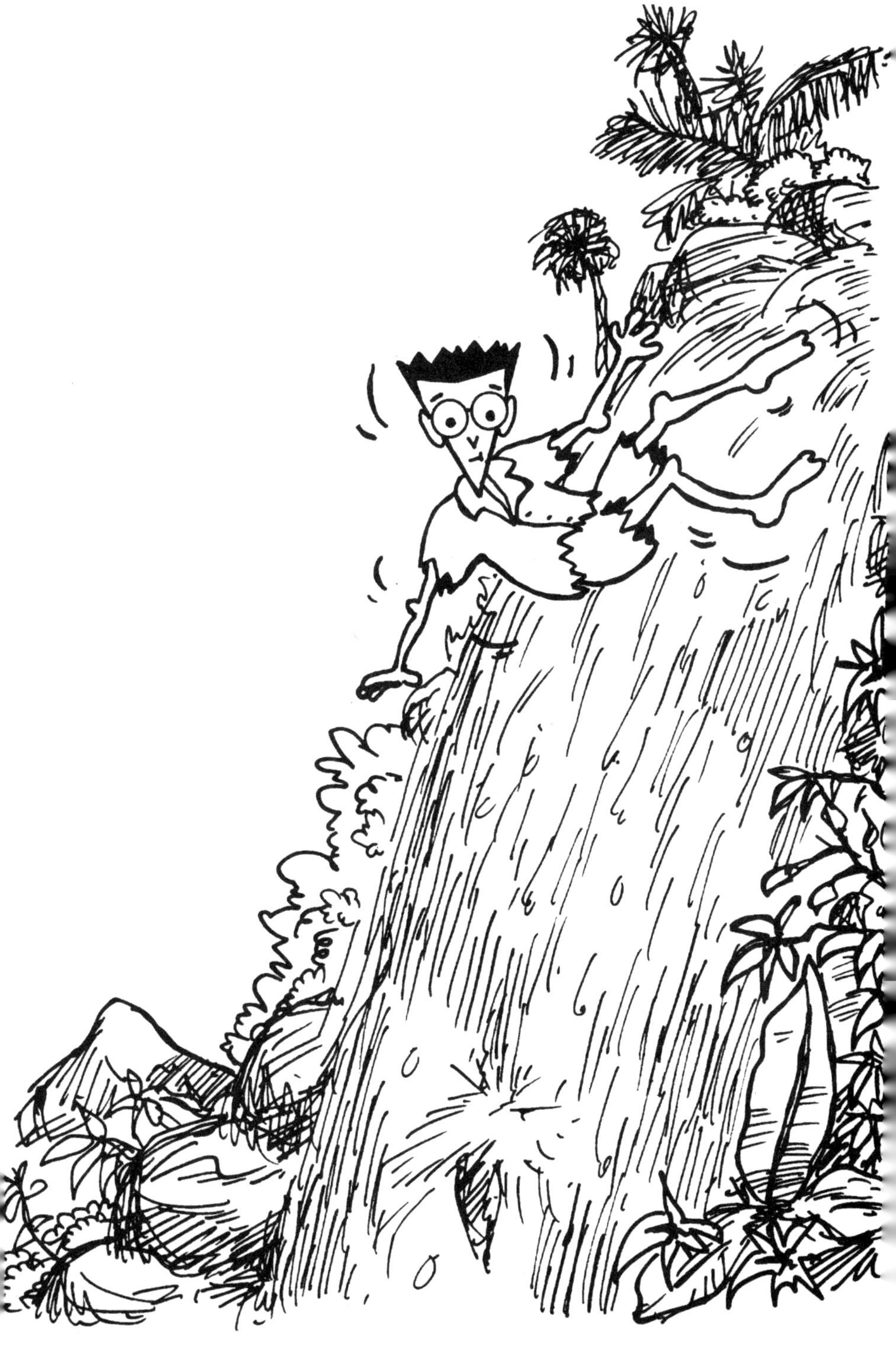

Chapter 5

Devilish DOS Programs

Paths through Peril

DOS and Windows are like two different worlds. One is the ocean underworld and the other is the land above. As to which is more beautiful, there is an ongoing debate. I guess it depends on whether or not you mind a few sharks once in a while.

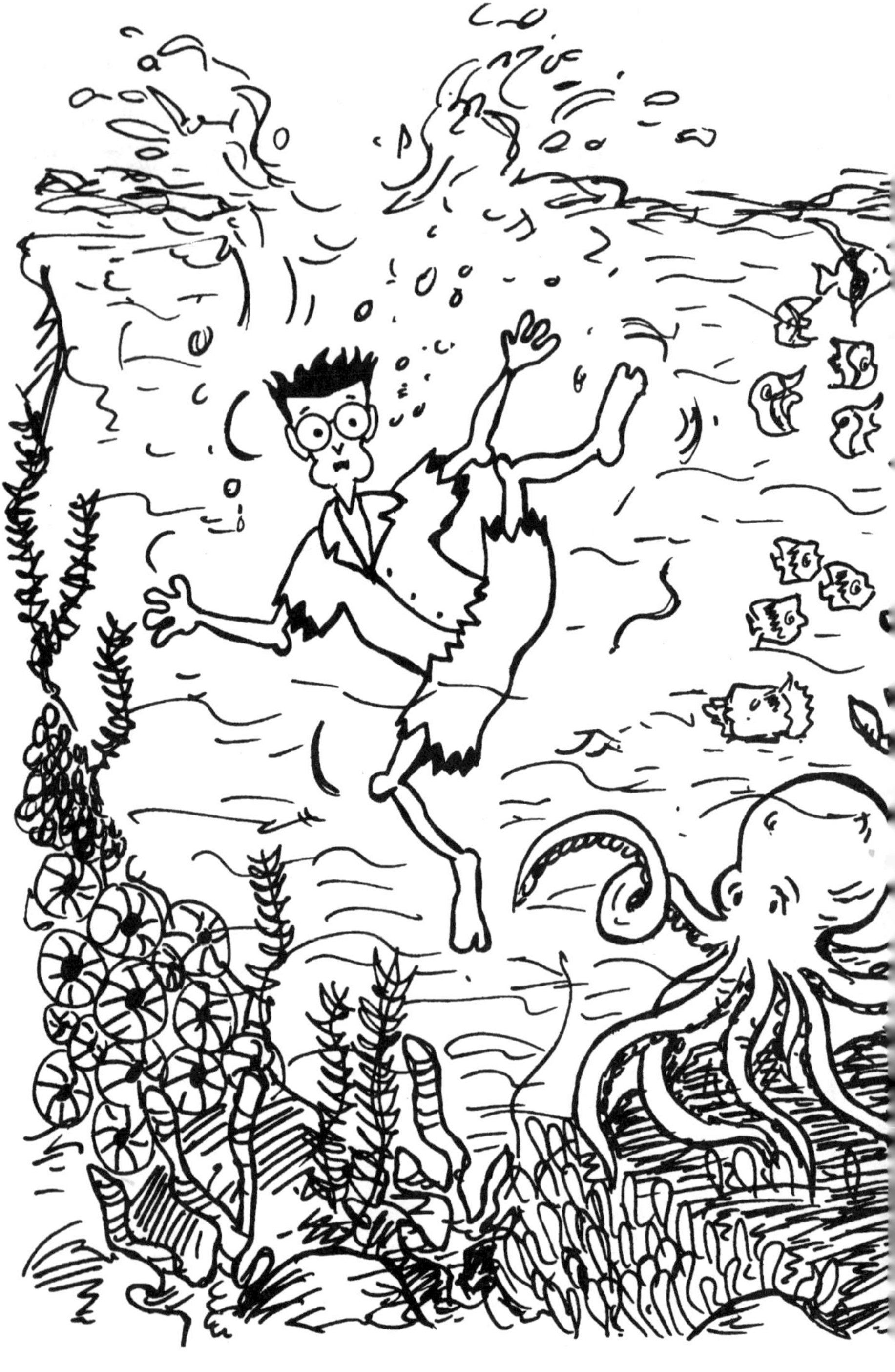

Devilish DOS Programs

As Winnie the Pooh would say: "Oh, bother!" This is a major inconvenience, to say the least. Just when you get used to one environment, you get thrust into another. Sometimes things aren't what they appear to be on the surface. And nobody seems to care whether you get a chance to catch your breath.

DOS Programs in Standard Mode

Poison: DOS program won't window.

The whole idea of running DOS programs in Windows is to window them, right? They are supposed to appear in a cute little window right alongside your other Windows programs.

Not on *your* computer.

Antidote: That depends on the mode you're running Windows in. If you're using standard mode (which means you have a 286 computer), the program uses the whole screen. That's just the way it is.

You can still open more than one program at a time, but you have to switch between your DOS program and Windows by pressing Alt+Esc.

Note: Running DOS programs in full-screen mode is actually a good thing because it uses up less RAM.

Devilish DOS Programs

No Way Out

Poison: Windows won't let you exit.

Enough's enough. It's time to shut this puppy down and go home for the day. You open the Program Manager's File menu, choose Exit Windows, and see

```
Application still active
```

Windows won't let you leave.

Antidote: This message tells you two things: you've still got a program running, and the program running is a DOS program.

What can you do? Press Ctrl+Esc to display the Task List and see what's still open. Click the program to close and click End Task. You may be asked whether you want to save the file; answer the prompt and the application is closed.

Now, get out of Windows and let's go home.

Forcing DOS Windows

Poison: DOS that should — but won't — window

You've got a 386 machine. Your version of Windows is running in 386 Enhanced mode (you checked About Program Manager in the Help menu to make sure). And Word for DOS 6.0 still comes up as a full-screen program.

Antidote: There's a quick fix and a longer-term fix.

> **DOS Programs and PIFs**
> Maybe DOS programs in Windows aren't all they're PIFfed up to be. If you're having trouble with a DOS program, examine its PIF file.

- **Quick fix:** Press Alt+Enter to force the DOS program into its own Window.

- **Complete fix:** Modify the PIF file for the program by changing the Display Usage option from Full Screen to Windowed. For more about modifying PIF files, see "You Should Modify Your PIF?," later in this chapter.

The DOS Clipboard?

Poison: Clipboard-blind DOS

When you are running a DOS program in standard mode, you won't be able to use your program's Copy command to put information on the Windows clipboard. DOS doesn't seem to know that there is a Windows clipboard and just sticks the copied data on its own clipboard, like it would if you were running the program outside of Windows.

Antidote: Don't even bother highlighting the text and selecting Copy. That won't get the data into Windows. The only real work-around (and it's still better than typing unnecessarily) is to press Prt Sc (your key may say Print Screen).

This grabs the whole screen — menu bar and everything — and sticks it in the clipboard. You can make sure it's in there by double-clicking the Clipboard Viewer in the Main group window.

You may have to delete some strange characters, but it's still better than typing that stuff all over again.

Devilish DOS Programs

Moving Data from DOS to Windows

Poison: Copy and paste trouble

You're running Windows in 386 Enhanced mode. You want to copy text from your DOS program to a Windows program. You select the text, choose Copy, and then press Alt+Enter to reduce the DOS program to a Window, thinking you'll paste the data right into your Windows application. But when you open the Windows program's Edit menu, the Paste command is dimmed. You can't select it.

Antidote: Seems like a reasonable request: choose Copy to copy something in one application, use Paste to paste it in another. But when you're mixing and matching DOS and Windows, you've got to take a slight detour.

In order to select text so Windows will see it, your DOS program must be running in a window. Next, open the Control menu and choose Edit, Mark. Highlight the text you want to copy and then open the Control menu again. This time, choose Edit Copy. Now the data is on the Windows clipboard (which is where you want it) and you can paste it into your Windows application. You can use the Clipboard Viewer, located in the Main group, to make sure your copied information really is safe and sound on the clipboard.

Note: At first glance, you might think you're having trouble with your mouse because you're unable to select text in your windowed DOS program. Windows is simply waiting for you to use the Control menu to select Edit, Mark. You can then select the text as necessary and use the commands in the Control menu to paste it into your Windows applications.

Squashed DOS Fonts

Poison: Squat DOS-windowed letters

You displayed your DOS program in a window by pressing Alt+Enter, but the characters look really strange.

Devilish DOS Programs

Antidote: You can change the way the letters are proportioned by double-clicking the control menu button (or by pressing Alt+spacebar) and then choosing Font. When the Font dialog box appears, try out a few of the different font settings (the effects of your selection will be displayed in the sample text box along the bottom of the window.) When you've got what you want, click OK.

Two DOS Is Too Much

Poison: Garbage at the Exit

After you exit the second DOS application, your screen suddenly shows a horrible mix of weird things. Not Windows things, certainly.

Antidote: In Windows's world, most applications look alike and sound alike. They do similar things. They treat your computer in similar ways.

Not so with DOS.

If your screen goes to garbage after you finish with the second DOS application, it's because both DOS programs sent different sets of instructions to your display card. And everything (temporarily) went kablooey.

For now, exit Windows and restart it. Now open the PIF for the program you were using and change the Monitor Ports setting to On. Remember to save the file before you exit. The line is

    local=EGA$

> **Techie Term**
>
> A *PIF*, or Program Information File, is a little instruction file that tells Windows how to interact with your non-Windows program. The PIF contains startup information for Windows about important stuff such as memory allocation, video mode, display usage, and output ports. The *PIF Editor* is a utility that allows you to view, create, modify, and save your PIF files.

120

Short RAMs

Poison: Out of memory (surprise)

You knew you'd be pushing it when you installed that DOS program. But you had to tempt the RAM gods — let's see this baby run!

"Sorry," says Windows. "Not today."

Antidote: You can do several things to get around a memory problem:

- Make sure you've used a memory manager like MEMMAKER to make the most of your available RAM.

- Make sure HIMEM.SYS is in your CONFIG.SYS file.

- Open the Clipboard Viewer and choose Edit. Clear the contents of the clipboard.

- Close any unnecessary applications.

- Minimize open windows.

- Get rid of the wallpaper by double-clicking Desktop in the Control Panel, moving the pointer to the Wallpaper options, and selecting None.

- Run the window full screen.

- Don't allow any DOD applications to run in Background mode.

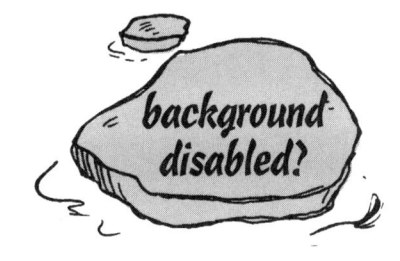

Running a program in full-screen size and turning off Background mode are two settings that your program's PIF file takes care of (see Techie Term in this section). Make sure that Full Screen is checked and Execution Background is not. For more information on dealing with memory problems, see Chapter 9.

From the Murky Depths: The Swap File

Poison: Can't run multiple DOS programs

Someone once told you that too many DOS programs would spill the bucket if you were running low on hard disk space. You've proven them right.

Antidote: If you are running Windows in standard mode, you have a good chance of hitting a wall if you use more than a few DOS applications. When you start a DOS (or any non-Windows) program, Windows creates a temporary file — called an *application swap file* — to store some or all of that application. The swap file is a temporary file on your hard disk. When you change to a different program, Windows sticks the program in the swap file, freeing up the RAM for other programs. Windows creates a swap file for each application you open, which means having too many DOS applications open at once can run you out of RAM and disk space (not to mention eat you out of house and home).

Where Do PIFs Come From?

Poison: Need a new PIF

Okay, you think you need a PIF for your version of WordPerfect for DOS. How do you make it? Or where do you get it?

Antidote: Here's the scoop:

- Windows comes with many PIFs included for various applications. When you use Windows Setup and choose Set Up Applications, Windows loads the PIF automatically and places the program icon in the Applications group.

- You can get PIFs from the manufacturer of your particular software. If you're working with a new version of a program, chances are a PIF file will be included already. Copy the file to your C:\WINDOWS directory (unless you've set up a directory especially for PIFs). It's a good idea to keep all your PIFs in one directory. If you have an older version of a program, contact the manufacturer to see whether a recent PIF file is available.

- You can create your own PIF files for programs that don't have one in Windows. Windows includes the _default.pif file that you can modify and save for your respective programs.

Note: You can create more than one PIF file for the same program, if you choose. Having more than one PIF file would allow you to start the program with different configurations, depending on your situation. For example, on days when you're doing the weekly schedule and have several programs open at once, you might want to allot only a small amount of conventional memory to the program. And on days when you're not working on the schedule and have just one other program running, you can give the program more memory. You could have two different PIF files storing each of these setups. One day, you'd choose the first PIF; one the other days, you'd choose the second. This keeps you from dealing with Out of memory errors and helps you run the program as efficiently as possible.

Should You Modify Your PIFs?

Poison: PIF-editing delemma.

Looks like everyone around you knows more about PIF files than you do. (You have these files only if you have previously told Windows to search for existing applications — either during installation or with Setup Applica-

Devilish DOS Programs

Words of Wisdom: MSD

MSD is a DOS utility that gives you a quick glimpse at the various components in your system. You can find out how much memory you have, what the name of your mouse driver is, the density of your disk drives, and the capacity of your hard disk, among other things. If you're having trouble running your DOS program within Windows, take a look at the way your system sees your system: run MSD from the DOS prompt. (You can run MSD from Windows, but the information may not be as reliable.) This may help you fine-tune your program setup, either in the program's PIF file or in the Windows Control Panel.

tions in Windows Setup.) That's all you hear — "PIF, PIF, PIF" — standing by the water cooler. When you say "My program won't window," they say "Change your PIF." When you have trouble loading a particular DOS program, they tell you to "Change your PIF."

What does that mean and is it something you should do alone?

Antidote: In most cases of popular programs, Windows finds its necessary PIF information by checking a file called APPS.INF. This file stores the best-case settings for most popular non-Windows application programs. This means that unless you're having a problem with your DOS program, the PIF settings are probably fine the way they are.

If you're having problems with memory, video, or program switching, however, looking at — and perhaps changing — your program's PIF file is a possibility.

To change a PIF, open the PIF Editor (in the Main group) and choose the PIF for your program. (The first part of the name may be the second part will be .PIF.) If you make any changes — and you should probably get the witch doctor's okay before you do — remember to save the file before you exit.

Runs, but Not in the Right Place

Poison: A program in the wrong directory

Well, it started, but it's running in the wrong directory. For some reason, the program runs in the root directory instead of its program directory. When you go to save files, the wrong directory always shows up.

Antidote: Two different settings control where a non-Windows applications runs:

- The Startup Directory: line in the PIF file for the program.

Devilish DOS Programs

🐟 The Working Directory: line in the Program Item dialog box.

If the entries in these two lines are different, make sure the one you want to use is specified in the Program Manager. Those settings override the PIF settings. To bring up the Program Item Properties box, press Alt and double-click the program icon.

Note: If you are running you application on a network, there may be other types of directories involved (in addition to the Startup and Working directories). Consult your network administrator or the manufacturer of your DOS application for details.

Anyone Care for Fried Data?

Poison: A garbled data file

More often than not, garbled data is caused by something other than Windows or DOS. Mixed-up, messed-up files usually happen because of a hard disk going bad, a diskette that got cooked in a car window, or some other physical happening. Even a power spike can zap a file; but not usually innocent little Windows.

Except. . .

Antidote: Display the file's PIF by double-clicking the PIF Editor icon (in the Main group) and selecting the appropriate filename.

There are two options in the PIF file that could cause a garbage-like display:

- In the Directly Modifies section, make sure Keyboard is checked and any necessary COM port is selected.

- No Save Screen should not be checked. When checked, the option tells Windows not to retain a copy of the screen in memory; then, when you switch away from the application and switch back, Windows is incapable of redrawing the screen.

Note: Some programs have their own screen-redraw utility. If your program is one of those, it's okay to have No Save Screen selected.

Can't Get Screen Shots

Poison: Clipboard doesn't see DOS.

Some people just like to take pictures of the screen, Windows is so pretty. They just pin them up on the wall. (And throw darts at them when no one is looking.)

Thank goodness you survived that one. Now it's time to head for higher, dryer ground.

Devilish DOS Programs **127**

You tried to take a picture of your screen and then paste it in a document you're working on. The clipboard wasn't cooperating.

Antidote: Here's another PIF problem. The No Screen Exchange keeps you from being able to take a screen shot of your display. That means you can press Prt Sc all you want, and nothing ever goes to the clipboard.

The good news is that you can turn this feature off so that you can get screen shots when you need them. On the flip side, if you're working with a RAM-hungry application and won't be taking pictures of the screen, you'll save a little memory by disabling No Screen Exchange (which is probably why it's off in the first place). If you can't paste screen captures, make sure No Screen Exchange is not checked in the PIF Editor.

No Deposit, No Return

Poison: Can't get back to Windows

You were starting to show off a little. Had to be the first one on editor's row to start Windows and shell out to Word 6.0, didn't you?

Oh. But what's the problem? You can't get back to Windows. . .

Antidote: Yup, broken record. PIF, PIF, PIF. Get out that PIF Editor and look at Word's PIF file. Is Prevent Program Switch checked? Well, it shouldn't be. Get that X out of there. After you save your changes and exit, you should be allowed to return to Windows.

No Paste-O?

Poison: Windows won't let you paste.

Similar to the desire to capture screen shots is the need to get that "something" off the clipboard. You figured out how to copy it up there from your DOS program, and now you want to paste it. It's a natural desire. But

Windows is ignoring your Paste requests, even though you used Paste just a minute ago, in Windows Paintbrush.

Antidote: Tucked far, far away in the Advanced options in the 386 enhanced mode PIF settings, you'll find an innocent-looking box called Allow Fast Paste. If your paste isn't working, your application should not Allow Fast Paste. Uncheck that box, save your changes, and go back to your application (not meaning to be bossy or anything).

Too Many Graphics

Poison: Memory problems with graphics files

Windows won't let you load this unbelievably lifelike GIF file you downloaded.

Antidote: It's no secret that graphics files eat up memory like an archer fish eats flies. If you're running Windows in 386 enhanced mode, there's something you can do to lessen the strain on your computer's memory, although it may not totally solve your problem.

Display the PIF file for the program and select the Advanced Options. In the Display Options section, make sure High Graphics and Retain Video Memory are both checked. Now, keep your fingers crossed.

Strange Displays

Poison: DOS program's odd display

Everything looked fine in Windows. But you started this DOS application and the display went weird.

Antidote: This, again, is a problem only 386 users have. And it's one only 386 users can fix. Open the PIF for the program, go to the Advanced Options, and make sure you've selected one of the Monitor Ports (you'll

What to Tell the Witch Doctor about Your Problem

Be ready to tell the witch doctor everything you know about your computer's symptoms as best you can (and with as little embellishment as possible):

- What apparently died/what problem occurred
- Any deathbed error messages it gasped before expiring
- When it last worked correctly (if ever)
- Any changes in the environment (office remodeling?)
- The last thing you did before the trouble hit
- Who touched it last
- What's been done to the machine recently (new software or hardware, new network connection?)
- First time, sporadic, or recurring problem?
- What you've tried
- What you think the problem may be
- Anything else you can think of

Don't be offended if the witch doctor asks you to go back through some steps you've already tried. He's probably checking for clues so small and technical that you didn't notice them.

probably choose either Low Graphics or High Graphics). Also, you *don't* want Emulate Text Mode to be selected, so uncheck it if an X appears.

My TSR Is SOL

Poison: A deep-fried TSR

You've had this version of Borland Sidekick from your DOS days. You're pretty attached to it. But when you try to run Windows on top of it, everything goes wacko.

Antidote: TSRs need PIFS, too.

Well, perhaps this is higher and dryer than you had in mind, but at least there aren't any sharks. There must be another way out of here though. Where on earth is that witch doctor anyway?

Windows considers TSRs "non-Windows" applications, which means the additional PIF information is needed so that Windows can be sure to put things in the right places. Even though you may be used to loading TSRs automatically when you start your computer, for best results, set up the application in Windows. Use Set Up Applications in Windows Setup, and then put the program icon in your Startup group so that it will load when you start Windows.

Windowed Lockup

Poison: Another DOS freeze

The program installed okay and put its little icon in the Applications group. You double-clicked the icon to start it and . . . the program locked up.

Antidote: Explore the following possibilities:

- The program didn't install correctly.
- There's a memory conflict between Windows and the program.
- The wrong hardware settings are specified for the program.
- The wrong display is selected in the PIF file.
- Try running the program from outside Windows.

Some applications cannot be run in a window, even when Windows is in 386 enhanced mode. These programs perform screen updates that conflict with the way Windows manages the display. Try modifying the PIF file so the program displays in full-screen mode.

Reading Smoke Signals

Like neon and tiki lamps, Windows programs and DOS programs are similar in some ways and different in many others. But if you're armed with the right tools, you can smooth out the way they interact with each other. And then, maybe, you can get some work done.

Application is still active

You'll see this message when you're trying to exit Windows and go back to DOS. The problem? You've still got a DOS program running. Switch back to the program (press Alt+Tab) and close that program; then close Windows the normal way.

Insufficient memory to run the application

This is a Windows message that appears when you are trying to run a DOS program that doesn't find enough RAM to start. Try raising the program's

Devilish DOS Programs

Your program cannot be swapped out

File allocation table bad.

Not enough memory to load

Insufficient memory to run the application

Application is still active

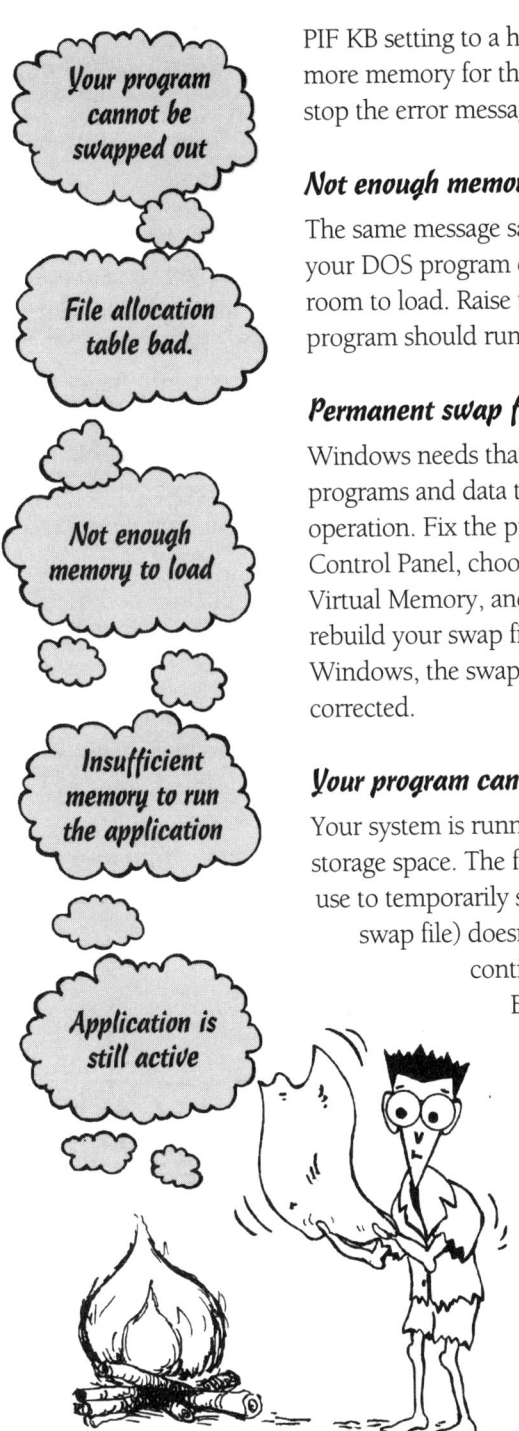

PIF KB setting to a higher number. That allots more memory for the program and should stop the error message.

Not enough memory to load

The same message said a different way — your DOS program doesn't have enough RAM room to load. Raise the KB allotment and the program should run.

Permanent swap file corrupted

Windows needs that swap file to store programs and data temporarily during operation. Fix the problem by opening the Control Panel, choosing 386 Enhanced, Virtual Memory, and Change. This should rebuild your swap file. When you restart Windows, the swap file problem should be corrected.

Your program cannot be swapped out

Your system is running very low on hard disk storage space. The file Windows is trying to use to temporarily store information (the swap file) doesn't have enough room to continue your operation. Before you can switch among programs, you'll need to make more room on the offending disk. Press any key to get around the error and return to Windows.

You Know You're Really in Trouble When...

You keep getting General Protection Faults (GPFs)

General Protection Faults are, as one witch doctor puts it, "Window's way of having a nervous breakdown." When you see a GPF, your system has crashed for some reason. GPFs usually have another message with them, giving you more clues about what's going on. You might see `System Error`, which tells you something is going on with your hardware, or `This application has violated system integrity`, which means your DOS program and Windows are fighting for the same memory block. In any case, get past the GPF, exit the application; and then exit Windows properly and reboot before starting the application again. This would also be a good time to turn on Dr. Watson.

You're running a DOS application within Windows and on a network and it keeps crashing

This is not the time to start flexing your newly acquired troubleshooting muscles. In fact, at this point, sometimes your network administrator will even end up scratching his head in bewilderment. Give him (or her) a shot at it though, and later both of you can make the phone call to the tech support line of the manufacturer of your DOS application. And when those guys answer the phone, be sure to impress them by being the first one to mention the word "PIF."

Chapter 6

False Fonts

Paths through Peril

Wrestling with Windows is hard enough — you shouldn't have to look good while you're doing it. But that's what they expect from us. Primo printouts. Snazzy reports. And just when you need its cooperation the most, Windows has a bad font day.

Disappearing Soft Fonts

Poison: Non-printing soft fonts

You installed the soft fonts following the instructions in the package. They work fine on one printer, but not on the other.

Antidote: When you install soft fonts, you provide a specific location — printer and port — for the installation. If you try to use a different printer and port, the fonts won't be there. Use the Font Installer and select Copy

Yeah, this place is a lot dryer. You seem to have wandered into a desert area. You've never seen this part of the island before.

Fonts to a New Port. The fonts won't actually be moved, but your WIN.INI file will be updated so the printer at that port will see the fonts.

Note: Soft fonts can be pretty slippery ground for new users. If you're not sure of what you're doing, ask the witch doctor for help.

Me, Small Font!

Poison: A no-name font

You're adding a copyright line at the bottom of your document. You want to use 6-point type. You're looking for the font you need, but Windows just keeps offering up "Small Font."

Antidote: With Windows 3.1, Windows added a new font — named Small Font — for the easy display and reading of small fonts. When you scale other fonts to tiny sizes (even TrueType fonts), there is a significant loss of clarity. Small Font was designed specifically for small type sizes and maintains its readability even when extremely small.

I Don't Have TrueType (Do I?)

Poison: TrueType unaware

You are just getting the hang of selecting text, changing the font, and messing with the size. You don't know anything about any TrueType fonts. Do you even have them on your computer?

Antidote: Look in the Fonts window of the Control Panel. At the top you see a list of installed fonts. TrueType fonts have [TrueType] beside the font name. If you have TrueType fonts installed, they will show up in the Installed Fonts: box.

Windows 3.1 automatically installs TrueType fonts, so if you're using 3.1, they should be there. You can elect to use TrueType in addition to your other fonts (that's the default), or you can tell Windows to use only

TrueType by clicking the TrueType button and choosing Show Only TrueType Fonts in Applications.

Foiled Font Installation

Poison: Font install uncertainty

You're not sure how to add fonts to your system. Don't worry about it — no one is, at first.

Antidote: Windows 3.1 lets you install fonts many different ways:

- The easiest: Windows does it for you. TrueType fonts are automatically installed and enabled when you install Windows.

- You can install additional TrueType fonts by starting the Font Installer and choosing the Add Fonts button.

Techie Term

Scalable fonts represent the high-end of font technology, allowing you to create characters in a wide range of sizes, styles, and personalities. TrueType is Windows 3.1's addition to the scalable font realm.

Raster fonts are fonts made of dot patterns.

Vector fonts are fonts based on mathematical calculations. And when you use TrueType, you don't have to deal with either of them. See your witch doctor for help.

Soft fonts are font descriptions in software form. They arrive on disk, just like a program. You install them and use them and, when it's time to print, your program sends them to your printer (a process called *downloading*).

False Fonts

- You can add HPPCL (for non-PostScript printers) soft fonts by making sure the correct files are copied to your C:\WINDOWS\SYSTEM directory (you need the AutoFont Support files). Then start the Font Installer and click Add Fonts.

- You can use the installation utility provided with third-party fonts

The Case of the Missing Font Button

Poison: No font setup, no-how

You want to find your way in to the Font Installer, but you don't have a Fonts button in your Printers Setup box.

Antidote: What printer do you have selected? Click OK to return to the Printers dialog box. Look at the Default Printer. Chances are, you don't have a Font button because your printer type doesn't allow (or require) additional font installation. For example, your Panasonic dot-matrix might not have a Font button; and your PostScript printer might not, either. If your printer required downloadable fonts or font cartridges, you'll see a Fonts button. Otherwise, you add fonts through the Fonts window in the Control Panel.

Printer Blindness

Poison: Printer doesn't see a non-TrueType font.

You selected a font in your Windows application, but when you print, that font is replaced with . . . *gulp* . . . Courier.

Antidote: Consider the following questions:

- **Did you change the selected text to the font you wanted?** Most programs require you to select text and change it to a specified font, unless you can set a default font for the entire document. Be sure you've got the font selected that you think you have. It's possible that Courier slipped in there without your noticing.

- **Can you print other fonts?** Try printing a document with other fonts. Is your printer seeing those? That particular font file may be damaged or missing if the other fonts print fine.

- **Is the font available on your printer?** Although TrueType fonts can be printed on any printer, other fonts are not so flexible. Make sure your printer is equipped to print the font you're trying to use. If it's not, the printer will substitute a font it *can* print.

- **If your printer is using a font cartridge, is the cartridge in all the way?** Some printers need font cartridges in order to print certain fonts. If yours is one of those, make sure the cartridge is pushed in securely.

- **Is the font installed correctly?** Did you use the Font Installer to install the font, or did you simply copy it over to your hard disk? Open the Control Panel and choose Fonts to see which fonts are currently installed. If the one

False Fonts   141

you want isn't on there, install it with the Font Installer (in Printers, Setup).

- **Does your printer have enough memory?** Memory problems can cause printers to do strange things. If you've got ten different fonts in a document and lose one, it may be that your printer is tapped in the memory department. Try reducing the number of fonts you're using and print again.

Even though Windows comes with only five TrueType fonts, using TrueType makes your font life a *lot* easier. TrueType fonts are available from all kinds of manufacturers, so if you think fonts will be a large part of your future, consider investing in a TrueType library.

Godzilla Characters

Poison: Bad-looking big characters

You had this great idea for an attention-getting headline: BIG LETTERS. That'll catch 'em, won't it? But when you print the page, the characters look worse than bad — they're horrible. Big blotchy things with blocks where blocks shouldn't be. What happened?

Antidote: This condition is called the *jaggies*. They appear because the font you're working with is a raster font, meaning the characters are made of dot patterns. When you enlarge those dot patterns, they look like big blocks.

Change to TrueType or ATM fonts, if possible. Because these fonts are not built on dot-to-dot technology, you'll get better quality in larger sizes.

Fickle Fonts

Poison: Fonts different on-screen and in print

You've finished your first publication and are anxious to see it in print. You've been bugging the guys in Marketing to let you take a shot at the company newsletter ("I can do lots better," you said), and now comes the moment of truth.

When the publication comes rolling out of the printer, it's a hodge-podge of character styles. You look at the screen. Okay there. You look at the printout. Definitely *not* okay here.

Words of Wisdom: TrueType

TrueType fonts are a new built-in feature of Windows 3.1. Granted, Windows comes with only a few, but there are hundreds more out there, available from other companies.

TrueType is the great thing it is because for the first time you can get an almost-exact WYSIWYG (what you see is what you get) display. The same fonts are used to create your characters on-screen and in print. And because they are outline fonts, they take up less memory than other types of fonts and can be rotated and resized to any size without a loss of quality.

All your Windows applications have access to the same TrueType fonts; you won't have to worry about changing the font when you move data from program to program.

Keep in mind that fonts eat up lots of hard disk space. Remove unused fonts and change to TrueType when possible. (Gives you more room for games.)

False Fonts

Antidote: The first question you need to ask yourself is what kind of fonts are you using? Most probably, you're dealing in raster fonts. There are two kinds of raster fonts — screen fonts and printer fonts. One kind controls how the fonts look on-screen, and the other controls — you guessed it — how the printed fonts look.

In order to have a printed document that looks the same as the one on-screen, you've got to have the same fonts installed for both the printer and the screen.

Check the instructions that came with your fonts for more details. You may need to reinstall one or both fonts. (In a pinch — or when you're aggravated to the point of setting your printouts on fire — let the witch doctor provide you with some magic font dust.)

Or, if you're just tired of messing with it, change all the fonts in your document to TrueType fonts (you'll know they are TrueType because they have TT beside the font name).

Uh-oh! Sandstorm!

Psyched-Out in Font Land

Poison: Imaginary fonts

Your system is in the shop, getting fitted for a new tux. So you get this loaner system with lots of cool programs yours didn't have. Look at all those fonts!

You decide to really wow 'em at the manager's meeting and create a report with some really snazzy font effects. You print the thing, and . . . Courier.

Oh, say it isn't so.

Antidote: It is possible for you to have fonts show up in your programs that aren't really there. Especially if you didn't install them yourself, don't be too surprised if what you're seeing are fonts that were removed (probably because of lack of hard disk space) eons ago. (It's kind of like looking at a star that burned itself out four trillion years ago.)

You've got two choices for solving this problems:

- Stick to TrueType fonts, which are designed specifically to be the same on-screen and in print
- Uninstall and reinstall the fonts you've got by using the Font Installer.

Before you do any major changing on your system, however, remember to make a complete backup.

Can My Printer Print TrueType Fonts?

Poison: Font-printing worries

You couldn't set up any additional fonts because your Printers Setup box doesn't show a Fonts button. Will you be able to print TrueType fonts?

Antidote: Literally every printer that can print from Windows — which is every printer supported by the Universal Printer Driver — can print TrueType fonts.

False Fonts

TrueType Alone?

Poison: Mix and match or stand-alone

Windows 3.1 installed the TrueType fonts on your system. Should you use only the TrueType fonts, or should you keep on using the cool artsy fonts you've recently added?

Antidote: Windows does allow you to use a variety of different fonts. You can still use your bitmap fonts right alongside your TrueType fonts (you'll know which ones are TrueType by the TT or [TrueType] beside the font name).

To tell Windows you want only TrueType, open the Fonts window in the Control Panel, click the TrueType button, and check the Show Only TrueType Fonts in Applications box. This ensures that you'll produce the

You just don't know how long you can carry on like this . . . There's got to be some water here somewhere. Where . . . is . . . the witch . . . doctor. . . .

highest possible quality on your printer and that the document can be printed on any printer type. If you prefer to mix and match font styles, you shouldn't have any incompatibility problems; do watch for low memory (caused by raster fonts that eat up more space) or printing inconsistency, however.

GPFs in Font Land

Poison: Unfriendly error messages

You selected the text, opened the Font menu, chose the font, and saw

```
General Protection Fault
```

What happened?

Antidote: Chances are, the font file you selected has somehow been corrupted. Exit the application (restart Windows, if necessary) and open a

It's so dry and desolate here. If only you had something to drink. Wait — what's that? You see yourself in the Sahara. And look — you have a canteen!

False Fonts

147

new document. Enter some sample text, select it, and try the font again. Same error?

Occasionally, a font file will become corrupted in conversion. Have you converted the font from an Adobe Type 1 to a TrueType font? Make sure you know which font is causing the trouble and then contact the font's manufacturer for a replacement font. Also, contact the maker of the conversion utility to see if they have a more current version that is more in tune with Windows 3.1.

Font Lockup

Poison: Font overload

TrueType seems almost too good to be true — until you pack a bunch of neat-looking fonts into that corporate report. Then, right in the middle of page 3, everything locks.

Antidote: How much RAM does your system have? TrueType fonts have trouble when there's not at least 2MB worth of room to play with. Your option if you have less than 2MB? Disable TrueType and use raster fonts until you can upgrade your system's memory. Or use TrueType fonts carefully — only one or two at a time — and stay alert for weird behaviors.

Changing Over Old Documents

Poison: Non-TrueType text

Sure enough. That vision turned out to be a cactus with glasses or something. Yeah, glasses . . . glasses of lemonade or iced tea . . . anything! Hey — there's the witch doctor — in Paris! Another mirage?

False Fonts

You have finished the first 100 pages of the corporate history. You've been working on it for months. But now you want to use TrueType fonts, and the rest is in the old font type.

Antidote: Well, it's not good news. Unless you have a third-party conversion utility that automatically converts old fonts to TrueType, you're stuck doing it manually. Oh well. It's brainless work — good for a rainy Monday morning.

Slow Screen

Poison: Agonizing screen updates

It seems like it's taking PageMaker forever to redraw the publication on your screen. You wait . . . drum your fingers a bit . . . wait some more. Oh — there it goes. Finished.

Antidote: Yes, slow screen updates *can* drive you crazy. Shaking the monitor won't help. Gnashing your teeth and swearing at it won't make any difference. So what can you do?

- Lessen the number of fonts you use in different sizes.
- Make sure there's plenty of room on your hard disk for a swap file (Windows may swap out fonts not currently in use).
- Free up as much memory as possible (TrueType likes 2MB, remember).

No . . . it's not Paris. It's poolside! It's got to be another mirage. There's the witch doctor, having a good time as usual. How come he never seems to be suffering on these journeys, like you are? The smug, cool, all-knowing witch doctor — give us a break. You're gonna die here, aren't you?

False Fonts

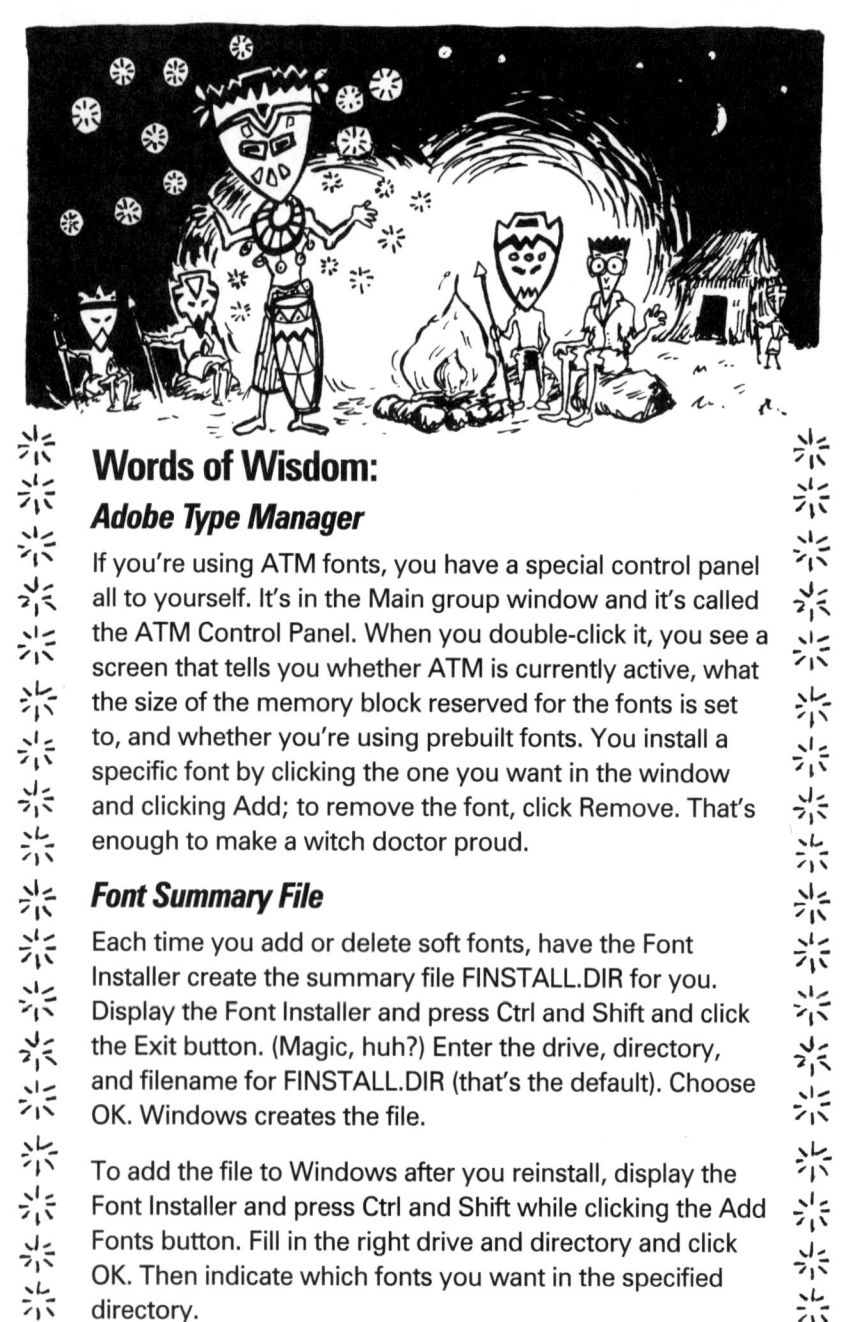

Words of Wisdom:

Adobe Type Manager

If you're using ATM fonts, you have a special control panel all to yourself. It's in the Main group window and it's called the ATM Control Panel. When you double-click it, you see a screen that tells you whether ATM is currently active, what the size of the memory block reserved for the fonts is set to, and whether you're using prebuilt fonts. You install a specific font by clicking the one you want in the window and clicking Add; to remove the font, click Remove. That's enough to make a witch doctor proud.

Font Summary File

Each time you add or delete soft fonts, have the Font Installer create the summary file FINSTALL.DIR for you. Display the Font Installer and press Ctrl and Shift and click the Exit button. (Magic, huh?) Enter the drive, directory, and filename for FINSTALL.DIR (that's the default). Choose OK. Windows creates the file.

To add the file to Windows after you reinstall, display the Font Installer and press Ctrl and Shift while clicking the Add Fonts button. Fill in the right drive and directory and click OK. Then indicate which fonts you want in the specified directory.

False Fonts **153**

🕭 Some applications allow you to turn off screen updates and then update the screen manually with a press of a key (like F9). Then you sit and wait for the screen update only when you *want* to. (A real sanity saver.)

No Room for Fonts

Poison: Running out of disk space

You've been running on empty for weeks, but you just *have* to have that one neat font and it's only available as a soft font.

Antidote: Font files, like any files, take up a certain amount of room on your hard disk. You can save a little space by telling Windows not to duplicate those files in the C:\WINDOWS\SYSTEM directory. That way, Windows will go and find the files where they are, saving you some hard disk room.

Natives! Here to save you! Yes! Yes! Please, don't be a mirage!

If you are on a network, you can leave the font files in the network directory and have Windows locate them there. Even if you are on a stand-alone system and you have fonts in another directory (so DOS programs can access them also), you can have Windows go out to that directory to get the information. To tell Windows where to go, open the Fonts window, choose Add Fonts, and uncheck the Copy Fonts to Windows Directory check box.

Monitor or Font Problems?

Poison: Bad or invisible fonts

When you were using raster fonts, everything looked okay. (Of course, *then* you didn't know they were called raster fonts.) You could read stuff on-screen. Now you've tried TrueType and you can't display your document.

Font Magic
Fonts can YELL!, whisper, (TELL YOU A SECRET), **State Boldly**, *look gentle*, Be 𝔇ramatic, and look businesslike.

What's the Best Way to Interact with the Witch Doctor?

As a being that's exposed to another realm, the witch doctor may be used to speaking a different language. Here are some tips for easing communication with your witch doctor:

- Describe the problem factually.
- Listen carefully.
- If you don't understand what's being said, ask for clarification.
- Take notes of things the witch doctor tries.
- Don't walk away — he may need to ask questions.
- Let him know how important or unimportant this is.
- Try to stay out of the way.
- Do what the witch doctor says *when* he says it — don't go off on tangents of your own.
- Remember that a little Thanks goes a long way.

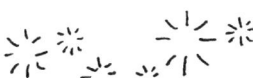

Antidote: Are you using a Windows-supplied video driver? If you've gotten your video driver from another source — perhaps the monitor's manufacturer — you may have trouble displaying TrueType fonts. Use a driver shipped with Windows 3.1. To change the video driver, go into Windows Setup and select Add/Change System Components.

Fonts Lost!

Poison: Reinstall wipe-out

You've just reinstalled Windows and now notice that your downloadable fonts are missing. All that work setting those things up, down the drain.

Antidote: When you reinstall Windows, you lose your soft fonts. This time, your only recourse is to run the Font Installer, recopy your soft fonts, and regenerate the PFM files (yup, time for lunch!).

But rather than letting this happen again, there's a special file you can generate that will store all the important font information WIN.INI needs. See the Satchel sidebar in this section for more information about creating this file.

PostScript Means No TrueType?

Poison: PostScript printer won't be True

Your PostScript printer won't print your TrueType fonts.

Antidote: Your PostScript printer has its own scalable fonts built right in. At print time, the printer uses its own fonts instead of the ones Windows uses. You can change this by modifying a few options in the Advanced Options box in Printers Setup.

Click the Edit Substitution Table button and, when the Substitution box appears, click Download as Soft Font. This "turns off" your printers internal fonts and forces it to accept the font instructions that come from Windows. You should see TrueType the next time you print.

False Fonts

Same-Name Fonts

Poison: Two fonts with the same name

Your new fonts just arrived. You tore open the package, looked through the manual, and realized that one of the fonts has the same name as a font you already use. If you install that font, your old one will be overwritten.

Antidote: Before you install the new font, use the Font Installer to change the font's name. Just select the font, click Edit, and enter the new name.

Note: You can't change the name of fonts stored on font cartridges.

Reading Smoke Signals

With the exception of a General Protection Fault (covered earlier in this chapter), there aren't too many error messages you'll see directly associated with fonts. More like reminders than errors.

Are you sure you want to remove the . . . font?

You are preparing to remove a font from the list of installed fonts, and Windows wants you to verify your action. Selecting Yes does not delete the font file; it simply makes the font unavailable for selection. If you want to delete the font file, click the Delete Font File From Disk check box.

No fonts found

You're trying to add fonts to your installed ones and Windows isn't finding the font files. Choose the right drive and directory and try again.

PCL Printing Warning: Soft font page limit

Your Hewlett-Packard printer has reached the maximum number of fonts it can accommodate: 16 per page. You don't have to do anything to get around the error — the printer will substitute a default font for the ones it can't print. When you go back in to your document, reduce the number of fonts you have chosen.

Watch for printer errors — either in your printer's LCD display (not all printers have one) or popping up over your Windows applications — that could be caused by font overfill.

Here you go. These guys know the way out. They say they'll help you find a way to attract a rescue team. Finally — some relief around here.

You Know You're Really in Trouble When...

Fonts aren't as dangerous as other Windows things, although they can certainly affect how your finished product appears. At least, when you're working with fonts, you aren't in danger of blowing up files or dismembering Windows. Sometimes, though, it's the little things that can drive you crazy....

You're housecleaning and you delete MS Sans Serif

Why is it such a big deal? Open a dialog box and find out. MS Sans Serif is the font Windows uses to create the text in its own dialog boxes. (Complete panic is not in order — you can reinstall MS Sans Serif from your original Windows disks.)

You remove some fonts and injure your non-Windows documents

Depending on how you've got your directories set up, you may have Windows programs and DOS programs you run outside of Windows that use the same fonts. You did some Windows housecleaning and now your DOS programs can't find the fonts they need. Chances are, you'll need to reinstall those fonts or allow your applications to substitute additional fonts for the missing ones (which not all programs can do).

Chapter 7

Printing Pains

Paths through Peril

You see the writing in the sand . . . you're walking into a potential pit of poisonous adders. Printing problems are perhaps the worst of all. You've floundered through this document, and now you just want to print the thing. And just when you think you've got one problem solved, another one slithers up.

Choosy Printers

Poison: Can't select printer

You've just created a document in your favorite word processor. Everything went great. The spelling checker worked on the first try, and you're anxious to see this puppy in print. You open the File menu, choose Print, and see

```
Printer: Default Printer (QMS-PS 810 on LPT1:)
```

You don't have a QMS. You don't even know what a QMS is. You've got this cool little Epson.

Antidote: You need to choose another printer. The printer currently shown as the default isn't the printer you're using. Is there a Setup button in your Print dialog box? Click it and choose the right printer.

Note: If your printer isn't listed in the applications list of available printers, you need to install the printer driver for that printer. For the necessary steps, see the previous section.

Unavailable Printer

Poison: Printer type not on install list

You went looking for your particular printer type, but it's not on Windows printer list. What does that mean? Will you ever be able to use your printer?

Antidote: There are two ways to deal with this one:

- The immediate solution is to choose a printer type that can act like your printer. (You might choose a similar model by the same manufacturer, for example.) You can also choose the Generic/Text Only or PostScript drivers, which are set to work with any dot-matrix or PostScript printer, respectively. Your printouts may not look perfect, but you should get *something*.

Printing Pains

🖎 The longer solution is to contact the manufacturer and request the most recent printer driver for your printer model. Be sure to tell them you're working in Windows (often manufacturers have different versions of the same driver available).

Whose Fault? The Default Printer

Poison: The wrong printer is always chosen.

The natives have suggested several ways to send out calls for help, but you keep getting no response.

Yes, that's one of the annoying things about installing every possible printer driver — the one you don't want may always appear in the Default Printer box.

Antidote: Get into the Control Panel and double-click Printers. See that list of Installed Printers? Your printer should be listed among those. Click the one you want to use as your default printer and click the Set As Default Printer button.

Now whenever you get ready to print from within Windows, the printer you selected will be chosen automatically. You can still select other printers by clicking the Specific Printer down arrow in the Print Setup box, however.

Dead Printer, Hardware-Wise

Poison: A not-printing printer

Perhaps the commonest of all printing problems is a printer that just doesn't. It's not moving. It's not flashing. For all you know, the little ham-

Printing Pains

sters in there are on their lunch break.

Antidote: The problem is usually a loose connection — either at the computer or the printer itself — or a kicked-out power cord. Check these things:

- Is your printer plugged into the wall or surge protector?

- Is your printer turned on? (And if it's a surge protector, is *that* turned on?)

- Are the cables tight? (Both ends)

- Is the cable in good shape? (If you can see the individual wires in the cable at either end or if the connector is pulling loose, it's time for a new cable.)

- Does the printer have paper?

- Is the printer's Ready light on?

- Could there be a paper jam? (Check for an error light. Unfortunately, if there's a page jamming your printer, turning the thing off and on isn't going to clear it. When you turn the printer back on, that awful paper jam light flashes right back on.)

- If you're sharing a printer with someone else by using a switch box (if you don't know what that is, you don't *want* to know), make sure the switch is set to receive data from your computer.

Gray-Out Print Command

Poison: Can't select Print

You're ready to send your document to the printer. You've spell-checked it and saved it. You open the File menu and try to select Print, but the command is unavailable. Windows won't let you select it.

Antidote: You need to choose a printer in the Print Setup dialog box. Some applications do this for you automatically by reading Windows's settings; others want you to do it yourself. Just click Print Setup and choose the printer you want to use. Then click OK. When you open the File menu again, the Print should be available.

Dead Printer, Software-Wise

Poison: A still-not-printing computer

You checked all the hardware stuff you could come up with. You even carried the thing down the hall, connected it to Shirley's computer, and printed a file.

Okey-dokey. There's something else going on.

Antidote: If you know the printer is working properly, something is going on with the software. For some reason, your program is not seeing your printer. Sleuth out the answers to these questions:

- **Did you set up your printer to work in Windows?** (Go to the Control Panel and select Printers. Click Add and pick your printer; click Install.)

- **Do you have the right driver for your particular printer, or did you try to install a "generic" driver?** The best fit is the driver meant to go with your printer, so contacting the manufacturer and requesting a driver is a Good Idea.

- **If you're using a DOS program in Windows, does your DOS application have a separate Setup utility that installs the printer?** If so, exit Windows and run it.

- **Do you have some other piece of equipment set to use the port you're trying to print from?** If you have a serial printer and have installed another device to use one of the COM ports, you may wind up with weird conflicts. If you suspect port trouble, dredge up the witch doctor.

- **Is the line SET TEMP= in your AUTOEXEC.BAT file?** Windows sets this file up automatically during installation, so unless you've removed it, it should be there.

Exit to DOS and attempt to print something directly from the command line. Press Ctrl+P, type a few characters, and press Enter a couple of times. Your printer should print whatever you typed on the screen each time you press Enter. (Unless you've got a laser printer, in which case it may just sit there and look at you.) Is the On-line light on? If so, try pressing On-line, then Formfeed, and then On-line again. That should print out the text you've been waiting for.

Remember to press Ctrl+P to turn printing off. If your printer still isn't working, something's really up. That's witch doctor territory.

HP Printer Trouble

Poison: An HP uh-oh message

You were standing around by the printer, chatting with your coworkers, when a light flashes on and the LCD display on your printer says

```
Error 20
```

Okay, what's that, and what do you do about it? (And do you have to put down your coffee cup first?)

How to Drive Your Printer

If you're getting weird stuff at print time, it could be that you've either got the wrong printer driver selected or you're using an outdated driver.

Find out the actual filename of your printer driver by going into the File Manager, clicking the Windows directory, and clicking the SYSTEM subdirectory. Open the View menu, choose By File Type, and enter ***.DRV**. Your driver files appear in the list on the right side of the window. These aren't all printer files — some are drivers for other system devices.

Your printer driver will resemble your printer's name — EPSON9.DRV, PSCRIPT.DRV, and PANSON24.DRV are a few examples. How do you tell what version of driver you've got?

Click on the printer driver you're wondering about, open the View menu, and choose All File Details. Then you'll see a line that looks like this

```
PANSON24.DRV    14592    3/10/92    3:10:00am    a
```

Notice the date. If you suspect you've got an old-old printer driver write down the date and the driver name and contact your printer's manufacturer. Or, if you have access to CompuServe, you may be able to get the driver you need from the Microsoft forum.

What's the Best Way to Avoid Bad Witch Doctor Advice?

Some well-meaning witch-doctor-wanna-bes can offer some pretty suspect advice at times. If you hear some of the following suggestions, you may want to get a second opinion before proceeding:

- "You're just going to have to reformat your hard drive." (This may be true, but rarely.)

- "Sorry, but your data's gone forever." (Maybe you can use UNFORMAT or UNDELETE.)

- "If you don't know what those files are, just delete them." (Those files may be network drivers — don't touch.)

- "Oh, just turn your machine off and on a few times." (Sometimes this is your only choice. Other times it means you just lost your only chance to save your data.)

- "Hit Ctrl+Alt+Delete or Ctrl+Break — that'll do it." (Yeahm sure. And it may send pieces of your file floating into hyperspace. You should do this only when it's a last resort.

The best witch doctors are the ones who aren't out to impress you; they just know how to fix your problem. And remember that even the very best witch doctors know when to say "I'm sorry — I just don't know."

Antidote: If you are trying to print a document with a number of soft fonts, don't be surprised by the Error 20 message. You've tapped out your printer's maximum on downloadable soft fonts. Just press Continue (which means that no, you don't have to put down your coffee cup), and the document will print without the wide variety of fonts you selected. Other more boring fonts will be substituted.

You can keep this from happening again by adding memory to your printer or keeping the number of soft fonts you use to a minimum. You may also want to check and make sure you haven't specified any soft fonts as permanent, which means they are always downloaded whether they are used in the current document or not.

Note: For specific, up-to-date information about using specific printers with Windows applications, read the PRINTERS.WRI file in your WINDOWS directory.

That's the Limit!

Poison: Petty PCL

Your PCL — HP-compatible — printer is being difficult. All you wanted to do was print this neat newsletter. You tried to keep the memory use down: you put all the fonts in small sizes. Your printer says "Not good enough":

```
PCL PRINTING WARNING: SOFT FONT
    PAGE LIMIT:
        Some fonts will be sub-
        stituted
```

Antidote: Your PCl printer doesn't want any more than 16 soft fonts. No way, no how. Your only recourse? Click OK and continue printing.

Bigger, BIGGER!

Poison: Not-big-enough PostScript characters

Oh, come on. The salesman told you that you could do all kinds of amazing things with a PostScript printer. Make letters as big as a page, if you want. What ever happened to truth in advertising?

Antidote: Actually, the salesman wasn't twisting the truth about the possibility. Even though the printer is capable of great sizes, many applications — and most you'll see in Windows — limit the size of your characters to 127 points. But don't blame Windows: it's the individual program's limit.

Out of Memory? Virtually...

Poison: Not enough printer RAM

If you just had more printer memory, you could do neat graphics and cool special effects. But a memory upgrade isn't on the horizon.

Antidote: You can get more out of the printer memory you've got by changing the amount of virtual memory your PostScript printer keeps for storing fonts. The current setting is the one recommended by the printer's manufacturer. You can find out how much memory your printer has by printing the TESTPS.TXT file (in the WINDOWS directory); then change the amount by going to the Advanced Options box and entering a new amount in the Virtual Memory (KB) box. Get your witch doctor's advice before making any radical changes.

Printing in Tongues

Poison: Weird printed characters

You're eagerly (well, almost) anticipating the printout of your report. It should look pretty cool after all the work you've done.

But when you pull the page from the paper tray, it looks like a mixture of Martian and Egyptian.

Antidote: The most common cause of mish-mash printing is a loose connection. It's possible for your printer cable to be loose enough to mix up the data but not loose enough to fall off. Push your cable in firmly (both ends) and make sure the thumbscrews or whatevers are tight.

Still not printing right? Go through the list and try these things:

- Is the right printer installed?
- Are you using the most current driver for your printer?
- Can you print from other applications? Try exiting to DOS and printing from a DOS program.
- At DOS, type DIR to display a directory and press Print Screen.
- Did you have the right font selected in the application? (Make sure the selected font isn't LineDraw or Symbol.)
- Most printers have a self-test you can run to make sure everything is working right. Look in your printer's manual to find out how to start the test for your particular printer.

If you've tried everything and you're still getting weird characters, try using a different printer cable. Cables take a lot of abuse in an everyday office environment; they get tripped over, stepped on, scrunched, and crimped. It's not impossible that one of those tiny wires in there has snapped (wouldn't you?). If your printer works with the new cable, you know the old one's fried.

Half-Page Printing

Poison: Half a page and then nothing

Boy, you've been waiting forever for your PostScript printer to produce something. Great things, these printers. Terrific quality. And they give you time to meditate between pages.

But your printer is even more slow than usual. It's like The Thinker, pondering its output. Blink, blink, blink.

When the page finally presents itself, it's only half there. You aren't going to have to wait another 20 minutes for the other half, are you?

Antidote: Chances are, you're trying to print a pretty heavy-duty graphics piece (or a document with an embedded art file) and your printer doesn't have all that much memory. What can you do to make more room?

- If you're using Adobe Type Manager fonts, increase the Font Cache to 128K or larger.

- Use fewer fonts, if possible.

- Check the options for your particular printer. (Find them in the Control Panel, Printers, Setup window.) You may find other possibilities that will help you save some printer RAM.

- Select a lower resolution for your printout. (Do this in the Print dialog box.)

- Add memory to your printer. But let the witch doctor do it for you. (And there's no point in your printer going under the knife unless you have at least 2MB printer memory when you're through.) If you're using a laser printer, you can probably seek out the manufacturer (a phone call should do it) to find out whether there is a memory upgrade kit available. Usually for a relatively small charge (small as compared to the purchase price of the printer, anyway), you can beef up the amount of RAM in your printer. Then you'll be able to print those mega-files, no problem. Wouldn't that be a relief?

The Big Printer Fake-Out

Poison: A flashing busy light with no results

This is another one of those quirky PostScript printer problems that happens only when you're standing poised over the printer, waiting to grab the printout and run to a meeting. Tomorrow, when you've got all the time in the world, the printer will spit things out faster than you can grab them.

It's the old "watched-pot-never-boils" thing.

Printing Pains

Antidote: Sometimes your printer has a legitimate reason for pretending to be working when it's not really doing anything:

- You're sending it a file described in another printer's language. (Make sure you selected your printer in the Print Setup dialog box. Just because you have your printer *installed* doesn't mean it's the *selected* printer.)

- It's got a graphics file that's too big to print.

- The document uses too many fonts for the printer's minuscule memory.

- The whole document is crammed into a few small chips and the printer is feeling overwhelmed. (Try to print the document one or two pages at a time — one if you've got special fonts and art.)

- The cable's loose.

- The Page Setup says Landscape, but the Print Setup says Portrait. Make sure all the settings in your software tell the printer to print in the same orientation.

If low memory is the problem, you can try printing the document at a lower resolution (if you can stand the loss of quality). To change the resolution, go to the Printers dialog box and click the Setup button. Click the Resolution: down arrow to see the available resolutions for your particular printer and choose the one you want; then click OK.

Note: You can have your PostScript printer driver print error codes by opening the Control Panel, choosing Printers, Options, Advanced and making sure the Print PostScript Error Information check box is checked.

The Frozen Printer Era

Poison: A printer that freezes everything

This is one of the worst of all possible printing problems — at least at the moment. After you've been working on that file, you go to print it, and Windows completely freezes. You saved that file, didn't you?

Antidote: Windows is suffering from one of two ailments:

- Not enough RAM
- Not enough hard disk space

You can free up unnecessarily used RAM by closing open windows and exiting programs you don't need to have open right now. You can free up hard disk space by deleting those publications you made for the Halloween Weenie Roast last October.

Why does Windows need hard disk space in order to print? The file is already on there, right?

When Windows starts juggling files, like open things and things to be printed, it turns to a special TEMP directory on your hard disk and says "Here. Hold this." Then it goes back to its other business. But that TEMP directory is a special place, and Windows needs to have enough elbow room in there. If your hard disk space is dwindling, make sure you keep as much room for TEMP as you can. Check AUTOEXEC.BAT to make sure there's a TEMP=... line and also make sure the directory actually exists.

Dead Print Screen

Poison: Print Screen won't work.

Most DOS things are worth groaning about. Print Screen isn't one of them. There's something kind of nice about being able to do a super-quick printout of something weird that appears on-screen. "See? I *do* have my report done," you say, waving a rough printout under your boss's nose. (**Warning:** Don't try this at work.)

But you improved your life by using Windows and now one of your few DOS pleasures is denied you. Print Screen is no-where's-ville.

Antidote: Windows has a bigger mission for the Print Screen key than just sending a couple of characters to the printer. When you press Print

Printing Pains

Screen in Windows, Windows takes a picture of the entire screen and puts it on the clipboard. You might not know it, but it's there.

Good news, though: you can turn the Print Screen key back on for your DOS applications by changing the program's PIF. (For more about PIFs, see Chapter 5.)

Likes DOS, Won't Do Windows!

Poison: Prints fine from DOS but won't print in Windows

You can print from DOS applications but get the Big Zero from Windows. Well, at least you know your printer is working.

Antidote: Windows isn't seeing your printer, for one reason or another. Check the following things:

- Make sure the printer is installed and the settings are right for your printer.
- Make sure the right port is selected. (Check Printers in the Control Panel to find out.)

- Make sure that there's nothing else in Windows competing for that port's attention. (If you have a serial printer, check your COM ports and other items like your mouse or modem that might be using them.)
- Make sure the line SET TEMP= is in your AUTOEXEC.BAT file.

ZZZZzzzzzz Printing

Poison: Snoozably slow printing

You've already been to the coffee machine and back. You've been thinking about walking back down the hall and getting those M&Ms that keep calling your name.

And your printer is still blinking.

Is it dead? Is it sleeping? Are you just supposed to stand here and wait forever?

Antidote: Minimize your application and double-click the Print Manager, which should be displayed in the bottom left corner of your screen. What does the screen say? It should show you whether your printer is active (if you see the word *Idle*, your printer is sleeping). It also tells you what percentage of the document has been sent to the printer (which lets you know whether you've got time to go get those M&Ms). If it says Stalled, click Restart and see what happens.

Reading Smoke Signals

Chances are, you'll know a printing error is coming before you see it. You're standing there by the printer, waiting for that printout, and nothing is happening. Deep down, you know something's wrong.

Cannot print

You could see this error when you are trying to print a piece of art that maxes out your computer's RAM. Close any possible windows and try to

Printing Pains

print again. (Sometimes saving and exiting applications, getting all the way out of Windows, and rebooting the computer frees up space you didn't know you had.)

Could not print page 2

You could see this error when you're trying to print a big (as in memory-hog) document and you're running out of either RAM or disk storage space. You may be able to downsize the memory needs of the document by reducing the number of complicated fonts or removing a few graphics. Another way to force a Big document to print is to lower the resolution (click the Setup button in the Printers dialog box), but you'll have to live with a loss of print quality.

General printer error

This is a "my-hard-disk-is-full-and-can't-process-another-byte" kind of message. Clean up your hard disk and try to print again. Make sure the TEMP subdirectory, where Windows sticks the print files while they're waiting their turn, has plenty of room to play with.

The printer on LPT1 is offline or not selected

Hey, printer, wake up! Something's not right — there's no paper, it's not turned on, the cable's not tight, it's not on-line. Check things out and try again.

You Know You're Really in Trouble When . . .

You have lots of opportunities to panic when you work with computers. But because of where printing falls — at the end of the process — you are right in the bull's-eye for a panic attack when you're standing in front of that printer.

You need this document now, and you don't have enough memory

If you've tried everything you can think of to get the document to print (one page at a time, lower resolution, fewer fonts, smaller graphics, reduced headings), try chopping the document up into several small documents. If nothing works, you can print the document to disk and print it from someone else's computer (someone who has more printer RAM, that is).

You have a color printer and no color

Your programs may be able to print items in color, if they have their own color printing capabilities and if the printer's software is able to interact with the program successfully. Just because you have a color printer doesn't mean you can automatically specify any color for any item you want. You'll need to run the installation software that came with the printer and check the manual to see what applications are supported. If you want to print color from an unsupported application, contact both the software and the printer manufacturer to see whether there are any drivers available that will help you do what you want to do.

Chapter 8: Multimedia Horrors

Paths through Peril

Life would be a lot easier if you could deal with things one at a time. But no. You have to deal with finding out where you are and discovering where to go. You have to worry about catching food and not *becoming* it. You're always dealing with a barrage of things at once. So you're used to multimedia, right?

The Invisible CD

Poison: Computer ignores CD

Your computer doesn't seem to know that the CD-ROM is there.

Antidote: Of course, Windows isn't going to see your CD-ROM if your computer doesn't. Here's what you need to check:

When you've tried everything you can think of to signal for rescue and nothing works, there's only one thing to do. The natives say, "Lets have a party!"

Multimedia Horrors

- If your drive is external, make sure the cables are tight.

- Your computer should load a driver named MSCDEX at startup. Reboot your computer and watch carefully for this message to fly by (press Pause to get a better look).

- You should have a MSCDEX directory off the root of your hard disk. ("What? I thought those were files from the previous user and I deleted them!")

- Make sure MSCDEX is included in your PATH statement in the AUTOEXEC.BAT file. Some systems require you to have a CD already inserted; otherwise, the driver won't load.

If you check all of these things and reboot and your computer still isn't recognizing the CD-ROM, give your witch doctor a call. It could be that the hardware isn't in right or something has corrupted the driver.

Windows Doesn't C D CD

Poison: Windows doesn't see your CD-ROM.

You toyed with the idea of adding a CD-ROM player for a long time before deciding to invest the extra paycheck. Now it's here and it looks great. One problem, though: Windows doesn't see it.

Antidote: Adding a CD-ROM involves installing a new piece of hardware and installing new software drivers to run the hardware. First, make sure the CD-ROM is installed correctly. (Most peripherals have their own test utilities that come with the software so you can try them out independent of Windows. Check your CD-ROM's manual to find out how to run the test.)

Words of Wisdom: Sound Recorder

Oh, you can do all kinds of devious things with Windows. By using the Sound Recorder (if you've got a sound board), you can record your own sounds, using a simple microphone. Tired of Henry sneaking in to play games on your computer when you're out to lunch? Record "Henry! Stop that!" with the Sound Recorder and then use the Sound Control Panel to assign the sound to startup.

If the CD-ROM is installed properly, make sure that the Multimedia Extensions have been installed. If they have, you'll see the media player and MIDI Mapper icons in the Control Panel and Accessories Group.

If you don't see the icons for those items, start Windows Setup from the Main group and install the additional features.

Spin-finity

Poison: A CD that spins and spins and spins. . .

The drive itself is working. You double-clicked the icon to start your new multimedia program, and the light on the CD-ROM came on. And you started hearing that whirring sound. And it went on and on and on.

Multimedia Horrors

Antidote: Sounds crazy, but almost every new CD owner does it at least once: open the door and make sure you've got the CD in right side up. The printing should be on the top. (Shhh. We won't tell anyone.)

Not Reading A (B) CD

Poison: Your drive can't read the CD.

Other CDs are working fine in the drive. You just inserted this new one, and the CD is just sitting there.

Antidote: Well, at least you know your CD-ROM is working. The problem could be one of these things:

- If your drive uses a caddy, is the CD seated in it correctly?

- Is the disk in correctly? (The writing side should be up.)

- Are you using the right kind of CD? CD-ROM disks are specially designed to store multimedia applications; audio CDs store music. Although most CD-ROMs will let you play audio CDs, you're not going to get data and programs off an Elton John CD.

- Could the disk be damaged? CDs look like pretty sturdy animals, but even they fall prey to unfriendly elements like high heat, dust, spilled cokes, and even fingerprints.

> **Techie Term**
>
> To have a real multimedia system, sooner or later, you'll spring for a *sound board*. This is a special add-on interface card that plugs into your computer's motherboard, equipping your system with terrific stereo sound. The most popular sound boards are Sound-Blaster and AdLib.

🢒 **Have you cleaned the CD lately?** Throw away that alcohol and cotton ball: the best way to clean a disk is with a soft cloth.

Simple Sound Problems

Poison: What's that? Can't hear you.

You thought it would work right off the bat? Nothing is that simple. You try it out and nothing happens.

Antidote: Getting that sound out of your computer can be a real challenge the first time. You're trying out hardware and software and Windows — all together at once. Let's narrow it down.

🢒 **First, is Windows playing anything?** Make sure you've started an application that is sound-ready.

🢒 **Are your speakers plugged in to the sound card?**

🢒 **Are you sure the speaker cords are plugged into the right port on the sound card?** The input and output ports look similar. Check your manual for a diagram.

🢒 **Is the volume on the card turned up?** The most popular sound cards have manual volume controls right on them, so you can change the volume right on the back of your machine. (You also can do this within applications, of course.)

🢒 **Are your speakers turned on?**

🢒 **Is the volume on your speakers turned up loud enough for you to hear?**

🢒 **Have you tried plugging headsets into your CD-ROM player to see whether any sound is coming from it?**

Chances are, your headache is something minor like one of these things. And there are lots of minor things to have headaches over. If you've tried everything you can think of, your conflict may be something a wee bit more technical, like an IRQ problem. In that case, it's witch doctor time.

Add Sound and You're Blasted

Poison: A silent sound board

Ah — at last. Your new sound board is installed, and you're ready to try out Dinosaur Adventure. Let's make this thing ROAR! You click the Dinosaur, expecting to hear a great noise, but all you see is what looks like a yawn. No sound at all.

Note: Some sound boards are configured for IRQ5 and cannot be changed. In that case, the other conflicting devices must be moved in order for the board to work. And that's a job for the witch doctor.

Antidote: Some things us normal people shouldn't have to deal with. Things like IRQs, or interrupts. Check the easy stuff first:

- Is the sound board installed correctly? Check your installation guide.

- Did you run the sound board's installation software? Again, check your board's manual.

- Are the Multimedia Extensions installed? You can find out by looking for the Media Player icon in the Control Panel. If it's not there, the extensions aren't installed. Use Windows Setup to add the necessary files.

- Is the right sound driver selected?

- If the answer to all these things is Yes, you may have a problem with your IRQs. To find out what IRQ your new sound board is using, check the sound board's manual or run the installation software again. If you're using a 386 or faster computer, try using IRQ 5, 7, or 10. If you're using a 286, try IRQ 2 or 7.

You'll know you've got the right interrupt when your sound board doesn't cause a lockup. If something else stops working, however, like your scanner or your keyboard, you've used someone else's IRQ.

Techie Term

An *IRQ*, also called an interrupt, is like a direct line to your computer's CPU. When one of the devices on your system needs attention, it sends data through one of those lines. Each device has its own unique line, and when two devices are assigned to the same line, problems result.

A Sound You Wish Were Silent

Poison: Ta-Das that won't quit

It was a really nice thing for Windows to include a few sound files right there in Windows 3.1. You can do a couple of cute things — ring bells at startup, play Ta-Da! when you close an application. You get the idea.

But you're trying out this new sound board and something is wrong. Windows looks okay, but from the moment you start up, your computer

Multimedia Horrors

plays Ta-Da! Ta-Da! Ta-Da! Ta-Da! over and over again until your brain turns to jelly.

Antidote: Now *that's* a painful problem — something close to water torture. For the moment — to fix it quick — open the Sound window in the Control Panel and, in the Files: box, choose <None>. Your computer is still playing the same sound, over and over, but the sound is nothing. Get it?

The larger problem is some kind of memory conflict. That board and Windows are wrestling for the same piece of RAM. Check the following things:

- **How much conventional memory do you have available?** (You'll need to exit to DOS and use MEM to find out.)

- **Is SMARTDRV.EXE loaded in your AUTOEXEC.BAT file?** Again, that hangs up some sound boards.

- **Have you used MEMMAKER or another memory optimizer to make the most of your available RAM?**

If you check these things and the problem persists, call your witch doctor. But until he gets there, keep that sound off!

Unsupported Driver

Poison: An unlisted sound driver

You've checked your hardware and software and come to the conclusion that this is a driver problem. Windows doesn't see the sound board because the driver hasn't been installed.

Antidote: Get into the Control Panel and double-click the Drivers icon. Look through the list. Your sound board's not on there? Check the software that came with your sound board — perhaps there were additional driver files that didn't load automatically.

If all else fails, contact the manufacturer to get the correct driver.

Sound Locking

Poison: Multimedia sound locks Windows.

You've just added a sound board and it works fine. But when you try to exit Windows, everything locks up tighter than Fort Knox.

Antidote: The software running the sound board and Windows are competing for memory. Try using your sound board's installation software again, this time watching carefully for any messages you might have missed. Some sound boards cause Windows to lock if SMARTdrive is in use.

Check AUTOEXEC.BAT. If you have a line that has SMARTDRV.EXE in it, try REMming out the line (by typing **REM** at the beginning of it). Then reboot your computer and try your sound board — and Windows — again. If that doesn't work, call a witch doctor for high-level help.

Why You Should Be Kind to Your Witch Doctor

Witch doctors have a tough life. They come when something is broken, they're under the gun because you want it fixed *now*, and they sometimes have to deliver bad news. Consequently, they take a lot of abuse. To make your witch doctor's life a little easier consider the following advice:

- Don't blame him for your problems
- Remember that behind the funky mask, he's human, too (although I've met some possible exceptions)
- Be nice while he's there
- Don't yell, scream, or swear at the witch doctor
- No hitting. No biting. No throwing things. Period.
- Thank him when he's done

Of these, the last is probably the most important. Kindness and sincere thanks goes far with witch doctors. Home-baked cookies go further.

Besides, you can expect to pay from $35 to $120 (or more) per hour for a professional witch doctor. So, treat the poor guy with some respect, especially if you are getting good advice free of charge!

Hello, DOS? I Can't Hear You...

Poison: No-audio DOS programs

Even though the documentation (and the side of the box) says you should be able to hear sound from your DOS program, you got Nada.

Antidote: If you're running a DOS application in 386 enhanced mode, you might get a message that the program can't use audio capabilities. Windows, in effect, is hogging control of the audio hardware and won't give it over to DOS.

You can get around this by exiting Windows and running the program from DOS. In most cases, that's the best place for running DOS multimedia programs anyway.

Are You a Player?

Poison: Media Player won't play.

Oh, you've got so many toys to play with. You've been experimenting with CD and sound stuff all morning. Now you're trying out your other Win-

Multimedia Horrors

dows gadgets and stumbled across this interesting Media Player icon. But it doesn't do anything.

Antidote: Media player gets a sound or video file you specify from your CD and plays it in the speed and sequence you select. Check out these things:

- **Do you have the right sound driver selected?** (Check the Control Panel to be sure.)

- **Are you using WAV files** (sound files Windows will recognize end in .WAV)?

- **Have you set the Media Player to play audio files?** Use the Device menu to do that. If you're trying to play an animation or video file and are having trouble, make sure you've selected the right option in the Device menu.

Techie Term

Another major draw to multimedia is the ability to add real-time *video clips* to your work. Games are starting to appear with moving dinosaurs, and one popular reference work includes real video of presidential speeches all the way back to Roosevelt.

Did You Say Something?

Poison: Voice-over confusion

Someone told you that you could yell at one of your coworkers from within a document (I think we did, in fact). Well, you want to try it and don't have a clue how to get the sound in there.

Antidote: Start with the Sound Recorder and make your sound (nothing disgusting, please). Remember to save the sound with a .WAV extension. Then open the document you want to yell from, put the cursor where the attack should occur, open the File menu, and choose Insert Object. Then choose the sound file's name. There it is, the little microphone icon. When Henry double-clicks it (and he will, because he's Mister Curious), he'll be in for a small shock.

See? Windows revenge. And who said Windows wasn't fun?

Fried Multimedia Graphics

Poison: Video blitz

You load up your new multimedia software. You're eager to see and hear it. Install seems to go fine, but when you start the program, your screen flashes a million different colors, with no recognizable pattern in sight.

Antidote: The program you are trying to run is not set up to work with your graphics card. Were you asked to select a graphics driver during installation? If so, reboot and rerun installation, this time choosing a different graphics card.

Some programs require a certain graphics type in order to display correctly. Check the software requirements before you buy. Don't purchase a program that needs a SuperVGA display if you've only got a VGA monitor.

Multimedia Horrors

Finally, check with the manufacturer to find out whether there's a driver available for your graphics card.

Slow-Motion Video

Poison: Animated agony

You've been hyped about this system ever since you decided to upgrade it. Now you can load up this new software and see real, live video clips from all over the world.

And they all move in slow-motion.

Antidote: Several different things can affect video speed:

- **The first consideration is the microprocessor in your machine and how taxed it is.** If you've got a 486 machine that operates at 60 megahertz, your video is going to move a lot quicker than someone running a 386 system with a 20 megahertz microprocessor. (Use MSD to find out what kind of microprocessor you've got.)

- **Make sure you've freed as much RAM as possible.** RAM considerations also affect the speed of the processing. Most multimedia programs are RAM hogs. Use MEM to check RAM availability (or About Program Manager, in the Help menu, if you're in Windows).

💨 **Does the program have an option that allows you to control the speed of video clip display?** If so, use that option to increase the speed. Check your program's manual to find out.

Reading Smoke Signals

The messages you'll see directly related to multimedia problems are few. In fact, unless you're trying to run a DOS multimedia program within Windows, you probably won't see any.

Device is being used by another application

You'll see this when a device you're trying to use (like your CD-ROM) isn't currently loaded in your computer's RAM. Check the Control Panel to find out what's going on and load any necessary drivers. You may also see this error when you're trying to run a DOS multimedia program within Windows.

This application will not be able to use audio

You must be running a DOS program in Windows in 386 mode. Try using standard mode instead. For DOS multimedia applications, your best bet is to exit Windows and run the program from the DOS prompt.

Multimedia Horrors

Error selecting drive. There is no disk in drive E.

You've tried clicking the CD-ROM icon in the File Manager, and either there is no CD in the drive or the wrong kind of CD is currently inserted. Check the CD and try again.

But it says Multimedia
Just because your software says "Multimedia" doesn't mean it will work with your sound board and your graphics adapter. Read the fine print on the box before you buy. And when in doubt, call the manufacturer.

You Know You're Really in Trouble When...

You make your system a multimedia system, and now you can't run the old stuff

Multimedia is fun, entertaining, expensive (although not as much as it used to be), and draining on your computer's RAM. The sound board and CD-ROM add more of a pull to system resources. If you're adding devices, add RAM. Also, once you get the system back, run MEMMAKER (with DOS 6) or another memory optimizer to make sure your RAM is used as efficiently as possible.

Your sound board fries Windows no matter what you do

You've tried everything you can think of, but Windows just fries itself every time it loads. You've got some kind of conflict, memory or interrupt. It's time for the witch doctor — or maybe even his witch doctor, the manufacturer's technical support line.

You thought you'd have great sound from a CD-ROM, but you've got these weenie little headphones

CDs mean great sound right? Sure, they can generate great sound, but can you hear it? Not with those $9.95 PC speakers. At least not in sterosurround-sound. Although computer CD-ROM drives are capable of things regular CD players are not (like reading art files, for example), there's no trade-off in sound quality. If you want to hear terrific sound, hook up some terrific speakers.

You keep getting Out of memory errors when you try to run multimedia applications

There's no way around it — you're cutting it too close to the wire. If you're starting into multimedia, 4MB is the minimum RAM you need. You're much better off with 8MB (get a few more if you can afford it). Again, make sure you've made the most of the memory you've got before you start that long trek back to the computer store (or to the boss's office, for a requisition form).

Your boss catches you recording "Take a hike!" on your Sound Recorder (and knows it's for him)

"Ahem. Is this what I pay you to do all day?" he asks, looking down at you over his prince-nez glasses. Go ahead, click that button one more time. "Take a hike!" Hey — *you* didn't say it; Windows did!

Chapter 9

Ready for Rescue: Memory Management

Paths through Peril

Ah, you're bone-weary and aching from this long, perilous journey. You've made it through situations most other humans face only in their nightmares. And there's one more stop — perhaps the biggest Window-hanger of them all: memory considerations.

How Can I Be Out of Memory?

Poison: Low end of memory

Memory, memory, memory. Everybody says you need it. But nobody gives it to you. Nobody tells you what to do with it. No one says why the memory you've got isn't enough.

Antidote: Out of memory errors pop up because the space holding your programs and files isn't big enough for what's happening to continue. The programs and files need more room, and more room isn't available. Yep — out of memory.

There are a few general things you can do when you start seeing `Out of memory` errors:

- Save the file you're working on, exit the program, and close up unnecessary files and programs.

- Exit to DOS, reboot, and restart Windows. (Sometimes Windows leaves little bits of files lying about that you can clean off by just starting it again.)

- Make sure you don't have any TSRs loaded.

- Try dividing your data files into small ones.

- Check your program's documentation to see if you can load a "lighter" version. Some programs give you the option of leaving off tutorial files, templates, and other optional necessities.

- Run DOS's MEMMAKER utility (or ask a witch doctor to help you) to make the most of your available RAM.

But I've Got 4MB!

Poison: RAM-rodded

You may have recently added to your computer's RAM. "That'll fix it," you thought smugly, sitting down to your first Windows worksession. Windows loads up okay, but after you get a few applications rolling, you start seeing the same problems you saw before you added memory.

What's going on?

Antidote: Even though your RAM total is 4MB, there may be several different kinds of RAM that comprise that total. Most of the programs you run in Windows are going to need a good helping of conventional memory (like 500K or more) in order to run efficiently (or at all). What you need is not more RAM. You need your computer to use its RAM more efficiently.

The following tools are available with both Windows 3.1 and DOS 5.0 (or later) for managing your computer's memory:

- HIMEM.SYS is loaded automatically to provide access to extended memory.

- EMM386.EXE emulates expanded memory or UMBs (upper memory blocks).

- Swapdisk manages the disk swap process for caching Windows program files.

- Virtual Memory Manager (VMM) controls swapping to temporary or permanent swap files.

> **Techie Term**
>
> A *memory manager* is a utility that controls and keeps track of what kind — and how much — memory you've got where. DOS 6 has MEMMAKER to help you make the most of your available memory. Other memory managers are available, but some conflict with Windows's own memory management techniques.

A Mode by Any Other Name...

Poison: Windows should start in 386 Enhanced mode but doesn't.

With your fancy 386, you should see lightning-fast Windows, right? You should be able to do all kinds of cool things that you didn't even know

Ready for Rescue: Memory Management

were possible (and probably aren't). But the thing doesn't seem to work any better than anyone else's machine. You look in the About Program Manager box and — guess what? The blasted computer is running Windows in Standard mode.

Antidote: If you're a brand new user, you're not going to care whether your system is a little faster or a little slower. You just want it to work. And unless you're working with DOS applications from within Windows (a process called *shelling out* by Those In The Know), you probably won't even miss 386 Enhanced mode.

But they told you it would work, and it should. So check out these things:

- **Is enough memory available?** You need at least 2MB for your basic Windows stuff and a total of 3MB if you're using DOS applications inside Windows.

- **Have you tried forcing the system to start by typing WIN /3 and pressing Enter?** If not, try it now. Maybe Windows is running in Standard mode because it thinks that you have a less impressive system than you really do.

- **If you reboot, does your**

Look! A plane overhead! You've got to get the pilot's attention. Who could be flying it way out here anyway? But no matter — they've got to save you.

Ready for Rescue: Memory Management

computer display a message like the following one?

```
Bad or missing
C:\WINDOWS\HIMEM.SYS
```

If so, your version of Windows is looking for a driver it needs to take care of memory configuration. You can EXPAND HIMEM.SYS from your original Windows disks or nicely ask the witch doctor to do it for you.

Pick a Mode, Any Mode

Poison: In what mode?

Windows started fine, but how do I tell which mode Windows is using?

Antidote: The Program Manager can tell you. Open the Help menu and choose About Program Manager. Not only can you find out which mode you're using (at the bottom of the dialog box), but you can also see how much of your system resources you are currently using and how much you have left to tap.

Techie Term

A *disk cache* is another mysterious-sounding something that can help you speed the way your computer reads in information. The cache is a small portion of RAM reserved for things your program is likely to look for. When it does, the program only has to look as far as RAM (which isn't nearly as far as the hard drive) to get the necessary info. Windows has a built-in disk caching utility, SMARTDrive. The file is SMARTDRV.EXE and should be loaded automatically in your AUTOEXEC.BAT file.

Mode Failure

Poison: Real or unreal mode

You recently upgraded Windows and sat down to your first worksession with 3.1. You aren't too intimidated; you already know the basics. But when you try to start that genuine antique Windows program (the one you love) in real mode with WIN/R, you get an error message.

Antidote: Windows 3.1 did away with real mode — use that only with Windows 3.0. If you just allow Windows to start up with the WIN command, the program will choose whatever mode is best for your computer.

Note: If you had a software package from the "old days" of Windows 2.X that you were still running in Real mode, now's the time to upgrade.

How Do I Find Out What I've Got?

Poison: Seeking out MEMs

It's hard to know what drivers in your system are eating up which portion of memory. You can say "I need to load DOS high" in six words or more, but doing it is a different story. How can you tell what's "high" and what's "low"?

Antidote: That's a DOS trick, the boring old MEM command. If you're using DOS 5.0 or later, you'll be able to get a world of information usually available only to witch doctors in-the-know.

First, exit Windows. (You won't get reliable information if you try MEM with the Run command.) Then, at the DOS prompt, type

```
MEM /C
```

The witch doctor? He has finally come to the rescue when you had just about given up hope. Hang on tight!

Ready for Rescue: Memory Management

to see a report of free memory for both conventional and upper memory, or type

```
MEM /P
```

to see a detailed list of how memory is currently being used in your system.

If you're using DOS 6.X, use MEM /D instead of MEM /P. And add > PRN to the MEM /C line if you want to direct the output to the printer.

Note: Do you do better with pictures? You can use the MSD command (remember that) to see a graphical representation of how your memory is being gobbled up. Just type **MSD** at the DOS prompt and then choose Memory. If you really get into it, you'll just *love* the information in *DOS 6 SECRETS* (IDG, 1993).

Slapped by the Swap File

Poison: Swap file problems

You've been getting memory errors and strange stuff. Someone said something about a swap file, so you changed disks. That didn't help.

Antidote: A swap file is a temporary storage place on your hard disk that Windows uses to swap programs and data in and out of RAM in 386 enhanced mode. Because there's a lot going on in Windows — especially when you have several open applications — it's important that Windows has plenty of room available for the swap file (Microsoft recommends at least 1.5MB), so it can expand as needed.

Windows 3.1 lets you create a swap file during Setup, or you can choose the 386 Enhanced icon in the Control Panel to change the swap file as needed.

The type of swap file you create can be either temporary or permanent. If you want to improve Windows speed, a permanent swap file is best because the file is stored in a contiguous space, meaning Windows doesn't have to look all over your hard disk to find it.

A temporary swap file, on the other hand, stores data wherever there is free space, which can require some hunting on Windows part. A temporary swap file is always created whenever Windows is running (with no intervention from you), and then it is deleted when you exit Windows.

TSR Trouble

Poison: No room for good stuff

You've got to have that screen-capture utility loaded when you run Windows; otherwise, you won't be able to take the screen shots for that new manual. But when you try to run other programs, you don't have enough conventional memory.

Antidote: If you're using DOS 5.0 and have at least a 386 machine, you should be able to load the TSR in upper memory. Make sure HIMEM.SYS and EMM386.EXE are loaded first, and then load your TSR by using the DEVICEHIGH= and LOADHIGH commands in CONFIG.SYS and AUTOEXEC.BAT, respectively.

Note: If you're having trouble with a specific TSR, take a look at the SETUP.TXT files in C:\WINDOWS\SYSTEM to see whether your TSR is listed. SETUP.TXT contains information on working with many TSRs known to have conflicts with Windows.

Which Mode Is Which?

Poison: Not sure about mode stuff

You're not sure which mode you should use to start Windows. It starts okay in standard mode all by itself, but would it be faster if you used 386 enhanced mode?

Antidote: There are very definite guidelines about which machines can run standard mode and which machines can run 386 enhanced.

If your system is a 286, you're going to be running standard mode. If your system is a 386 and you've got at least 1MB (preferably 2MB) of RAM available, you'll wind up in 386 enhanced mode. If you have a machine capable of 386 enhanced mode, you can force Windows to start in standard mode by typing the WIN /S startup command.

Note: Most people find that for simple single-application Windows use, there's no great difference between standard and 386 enhanced mode. The primary difference comes when you want to run many applications at once or window non-Windows applications (as opposed to running them in full-screen size). If you're using lots of Windows applications, run Standard mode. For the best in DOS application support, choose 386 Enhanced mode.

Loading Drivers: Oh No, I Won't!

Poison: Uncooperative drivers

Uh-oh! Bad news! Engine trouble. . . .

Ready for Rescue: Memory Management

You're trying to load your device drivers into upper memory. You think you've got the process right. But they just won't go.

Antidote: Those drivers (or programs, for that matter) should load into upper memory if you're using a 386 and

- You've got more than 1MB total RAM.
- CONFIG.SYS loads HIMEM.SYS before any other DEVICE command.
- CONFIG.SYS includes, after HIMEM.SYS, EMM386.EXE (with the NOEMS or the RAM switch).
- CONFIG.SYS loads HIMEM.SYS amd EMM386.EXE before any DEVICEHIGH command.
- You use a DEVICEHIGH= command for each driver.

You Know You Need More Memory When...
You can't play Solitaire with your word processing running.
You forgot your lunch three times this week.
You can't cut and paste.
Nothing starts.
You can't remember when payday is.

RAM! I Need More RAM!

Poison: Drained extended memory

You don't have enough extended memory to run the things you want to run.

Antidote: Try these things to free up more extended memory:

- Check the program requirements and make sure you've got enough physical memory to meet that requirement (for example, if you need 4MB and you've only got 2MB installed, no amount of juggling is going to give you the extra memory you need).

- Open CONFIG.SYS and look at the DEVICE lines for RAMDrive and EMM386. You can try reducing the amount of memory allotted to these programs (but you should ask the witch doctor first, just to make sure).

- Look through AUTOEXEC.BAT and CONFIG.SYS to make sure they don't load any programs that use extended memory unnecessarily.

Reading Smoke Signals

Abnormal termination

The Windows program you're using doesn't have enough memory to continue. Exit to DOS and try to free up more memory before restarting the application.

Insufficient conventional memory

Again, another form of error message, this one tells you that you don't have enough conventional memory. Remove any unnecessary programs or drivers and be sure to use a memory optimizer like DOS 6's MEMMAKER.

Ready for Rescue: Memory Management **215**

Thought bubbles (left margin):
- Abnormal termination
- Unable to start Enhanced Mode
- Insufficient conventional memory
- Cannot start Windows in Standard Mode
- Abnormal termination

Unable to start Enhanced Mode

Your system tried to start in 386 enhanced mode but didn't have enough memory to load the program. You can try starting Windows in standard mode by using WIN /S, but check CONFIG.SYS first to see whether EMM386.EXE is loaded automatically. If it is, add REM in front of the line (use any text editor, like Windows Notepad) and save the file. After you reboot, you can try to start Windows in standard mode.

You Know You're Really in Trouble When...

You don't have the minimum requirements to start Windows in standard mode

Adding system memory these days is a fairly simple thing to do. Not unreachably expensive, and not impossible to get done (or even do yourself). Remember, though, that if you're planning on adding memory, you may as well bring your total RAM up to 4MB (or even 8, if you've been saving your pennies). That way, it will be many moons before you have to worry about memory issues again (and won't that be *nice*?).

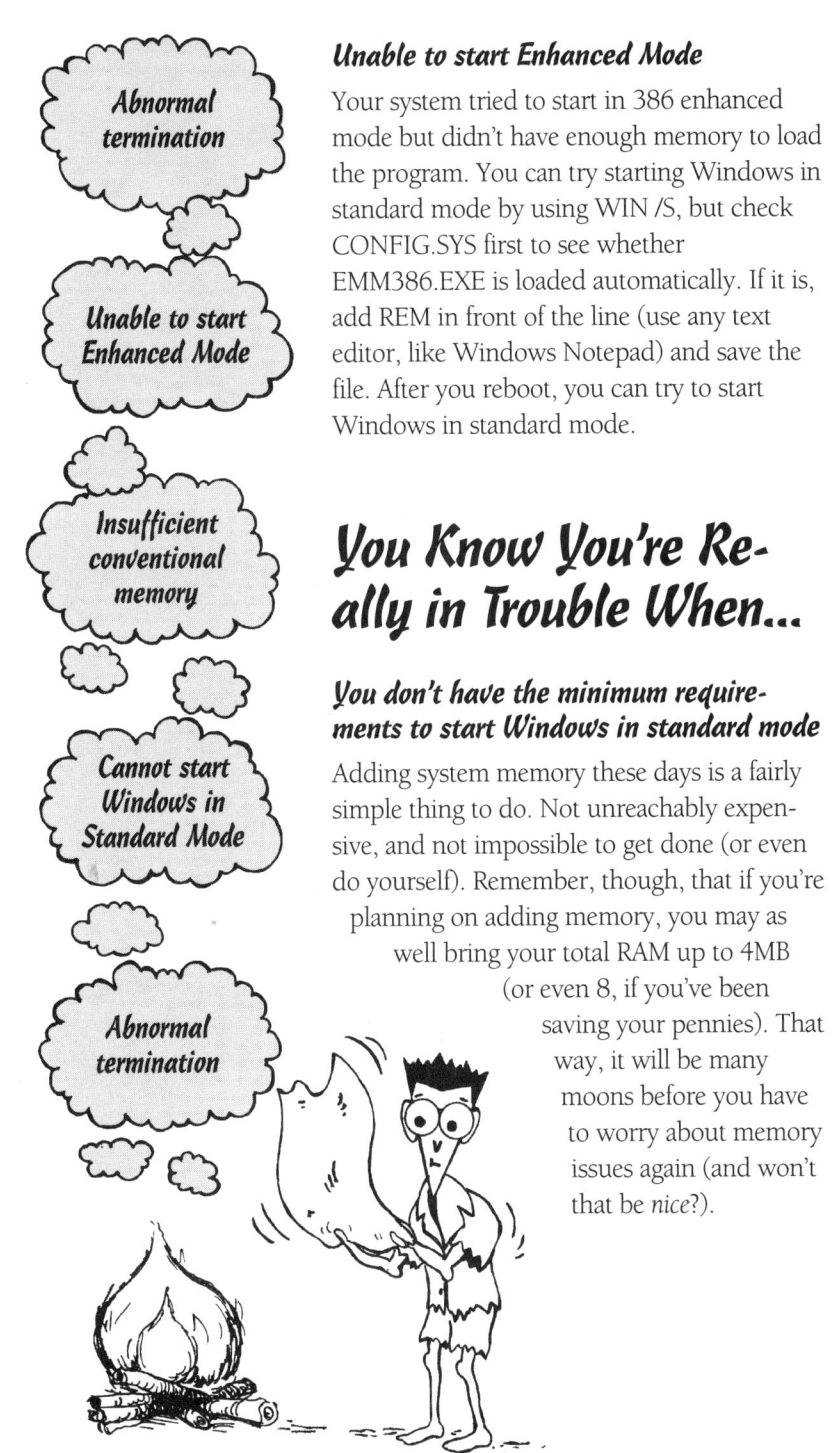

The pilot is unusually calm as he says, "Grab your parachute folks — we're going down. . . ."

Epilogue

O h, the stories you'll have to tell when this experience is over. They'll be boring grandchildren for generations to come. Twenty years from now, your Windows-wrestling feats will seem incredible. When multimedia, neural networks, and virtual reality fall by the wayside, all to be replaced by a brand of technology that we can now only imagine.

But there will always be witch doctors.

And there will always be those of us who feel stranded — cast away — by the rapid pace of it all, thrown into some kind of high-tech rat race with time. Sometimes, it's by choice, but too often all of this technology is imposed upon us. And in a sea of company procedure, policy, and politics, we are somehow left alone. Yes, set adrift in a sea of technology, with the human element distinctly no where to be found.

Take heart, though, because things have a way of coming around again. The pendulum swings this way and that. But it always comes back again. This week you'll be learning WordPerfect, and next week it'll be Excel. Tomorrow, who knows? But this much is for certain: There will always be folks who are willing to help each other — through it all.

An S.O.S. book may get you through this time, but don't worry, you'll find your own witch doctors. In the meantime, I've gathered together some advice from some of the best that we were able to track down. Sure, it's kind of general and philosophical, and it may not seem to relate to your problems much right now; but you'd be surprised. These are the secrets that every good witch doctor abides by. Study them. Learn to feel them, live them, breathe them.

There are at least a few of you out there who someday are going to be witch doctors, too. (Don't laugh; I'm not kidding.)

When Should You Call the Witch Doctor?

This is a personal decision. The range of choices runs from anytime to never. Take your pick. I'd say that it's safe to say that when you've run out of possibilities of your own for solving a problem, it's probably a good time to start.

Beyond that, think about the costs and benefits. State-of-the-art advice can be very expensive, and free advice can turn out to be very expensive, too. The most important thing you can do is become a proactive learner of the technology that confronts you. Apparently, you are, or you wouldn't be here. So, congratulations. I think you're on the right track.

So, What Do the Scrolls Mean?

I thought you'd ask. Here's what all of those hints were about in the DOS Island journey. Again, study them. A little troubleshooting theory isn't going to kill you.

Isolate the problem

Isolating the problem means finding what's *really* wrong. Many times, the surface symptom ("I just turned it on and it said 'Non-system disk or disk error.' Is my hard drive gone?") may or may not be the ultimate

Epilogue

problem ("Hey! Who left this floppy disk in my computer?"). The trick to troubleshooting is finding and fixing *problems*, not *symptoms*. It's a process. One step and then another. Change one thing, try again. Pick a spot and troubleshoot in one direction. Isolate the problem and then solve it. One trick is to follow the power source. Follow the path of electricity. Follow the path of information. Rule out possible causes each step along the way.

Start Over and Try Again

The simplest case is: Turn it off. Wait a few seconds. Turn it back on. And try again. You would be amazed how may times this works. Who cares why. It just does.

When you have a problem. Go back to the beginnning. Retrace your steps. Things may not be as they had seemed when you first got into the mess.

Always Have a Backup

There's an old computer saying that goes like this: "There are two kinds of people in the world: those whose hard drives have failed on them and those whose haven't — yet." It's a real gem, isn't it? The saying is very true (everyone who's lost a drive is sagely nodding right now). If you're one of the lucky ones whose drive is still running, *now* is the time to learn about backups. Start today, right now, this minute — before it's too late.

Many application programs have an "autosave" feature which helps when you're deeply focused on "creating" and kinda-sorta forgot to save that document you just worked on all morning. If you've got this option, use it! Startup disks are something else you just can't have enough of. You should have at least one (preferably two) System Survival Disks handy at all times. Back up your passwords, too. If you're working with password-protected files, seal your password in an envelope and give it to your boss or other trusted coworker.

The simplest data backups involve copying things to floppy disks as you create them. For example, when you finish a document in your word processor, take a second and use the Save As command (or whatever it is in your particular package) to put a copy on a diskette. Save the original on the hard drive. To make the data *much* safer, take the disk home with you each night and bring it back the following day. Backups don't do much good if they're sitting next to the computer while the building burns down around them.

More complex and larger backups usually require extra accessories for your computer. The most common item is a tape backup system. It's common to use more than one tape when you back up this way. With two tapes, you'd use Tape #1 this week and Tape #2 next week. The third week, go back to Tape #1. This way, you always have a backup for your backup.

Backups are funny things. If you never need them, dealing with them seems like more of a pain than it's worth. When the time comes (and it will), you'll look like a hero. Put some serious time and effort into designing a backup system for your computer. If your PC is your lifeblood, find a witch doctor to get you set up. Remember that you're doing this for yourself — a backup is personal insurance that *will* pay off; the only question is when.

Know How to Undo Things

So here you are: something bad happened and you want to go back in time to the point before whatever-it-is went wrong. In short, you want to *undo* the crisis. Undo is one of those techno-philosophical concepts that keeps many nerds going at 3 a.m. and many Chinese restaurants flush with late-night business.

Depending on your situation, "undo" can have many forms. Conceptually, you're trying to reverse or otherwise bail out of a bad situation. Here are some ideas to get you out of whatever dire straights you've gotten yourself into:

- **Keep a current backup.** A good backup is the ultimate "undo."

- **Quit without saving.** Almost every program known to mankind has an almost neurotic desire to save your changes. What if you don't *want* to save them? Close the file or quit the program. When it asks if you want to save those all-important changes, say no. Voilà! You're right back to where you started.

Epilogue

- **Try Undo.** The Undo command traditionally lets you escape the consequences of whatever heinous software crime you've committed, but ONLY your most recent one. Multiple heinous software crimes are beyond the forgiving capacities of Undo; seek solace from Quit without Saving.

- **Escape, Ctrl-C, and Ctrl-Break.** These are DOS-level tricks (although Escape often works in application programs too!). If you typed **FORMAT C:** just to see what it looked like sitting there on the command line and are now too terrified to move, press any of these keys. They tell DOS to ignore what's on the command line (Escape) or stop whatever it's trying to do right now (Ctrl-C or Ctrl-Break). By the way, they're in order by strength. Often, Ctrl-Break will get you out of a bind that the other two won't seem to affect.

- **Beware of programs that make changes for you.** Many installation routines "help" you by posting changes to your CONFIG.SYS and AUTOEXEC.BAT files (and WIN.INI for Windows programs). Granted, they usually warn you of what they're about to do, but it's still not the same as a qualified witch doctor inserting the same changes. If things don't work right after the automated surgery, look for the backup copies of these files.

- **Look for automatic .BAK files.** Some programs (such as Microsoft Word) automatically make backup files for you.

Don't Make Assumptions

Believe it or not, this is what separates decent troubleshooters from Great Witch Doctors. If you master it, it will have the same effect on your computing future. When you're trying to resolve something, watch out for your assumptions. Like blinders that limit your vision, they can send you off on wild-goose chases, snipe hunts, Congressional fact-finding junkets, and other wastes of time. Incorrect assumptions can even *prevent* you from finding the correct answer. How do you avoid this?

- Don't get focused on "the answer" too soon. Sometimes a problem appears that you've dealt with before. You immediately implement your tried-and-true solution, which doesn't work this time. After spending time and effort chasing an assumed problem, you've still got the real problem left to solve. Using previous experience is vital, but always leave your mind open to new twists on old plots.

- Separate obvious symptoms from hidden problems. This goes back to good troubleshooting technique.

- Don't assume it's *really* a problem. Many, many "problems" are solved by just turning the stupid machine off and on again. Try it. Keep in mind that the average 386 is doing a few million things *per second*. If it runs without a hitch for one minute, it's done *several hundred million* consecutive things right. If it screws up once in a while, who could blame it? Restart and then give it a chance to try again.

- Look for the right things. If you're having an "I've lost something" crisis, don't assume you're looking in the right place. Make sure you've got the right *file* in the right *directory* on the right *disk*.

- Don't assume any one step is working. Think through the process step by step. Things you skipped because you assumed them to be correct can be your downfall. Check and then check again.

- Don't assume the blame yet; it may not be your fault. When something in your computer does the electronic equivalent of going "ping," it's perfectly normal (if not factually correct) to blurt out "I broke it. I killed it. It's all my fault." Many times, *you* didn't break it. It just broke. Don't jump on yourself too quickly.

If you *did* do it, learn from the experience. Keep your perspective. These things are never *that* tragic — really. Don't verbally berate yourself into a high blood pressure prescription; it's just not worth it.

Epilogue

Don't Panic

"Format complete," the screen sadistically chirps. A thick veil lifts from your consciousness and you wonder, "Format of *what* is complete? Was I *formatting* something?!?" Your stress level begins an inexorable climb as you remember all those silly questions the computer rather unexpectedly asked you a few minutes ago (the ones like "All data will be erased. OK to proceed?" and the almighty "Are you sure?"). Did they really *mean* something? Visions flash before your eyes: spreadsheets predicting the financial future of your world, Pulitzer prize-winning justification memos, that super-cool jet fighter game with the high score in your name. Your eyes grow wide and the index finger on your left hand begins to involuntarily twitch.

This is *panic*. And panic-stricken people do not operate computers very well.

Bury what I'm about to say deep in your subconscious where it can fight its way to the surface when your brain hits the panic button: *get up and get away*. Put a little sign on the computer that says "having a bad hair day" and walk out of there for a few minutes. Get all the emotion out of your system and regain logical control before you even think about sitting down at your computer again. This *will* be hard, but you'll thank me later.

When it's time for your moment like this, remember that madly thrashing around trying to "fix" whatever crisis you're having will probably do more damage than the crisis itself entails. Almost any problem can be solved, provided a logical, rational mind is at the helm. If you think the problem is that big, call someone before you try anything. Panic throws everything out of proportion, making even the smallest of problems look like a disaster. Just go somewhere and settle down. When you're approximating normalcy again, have another look at your computer.

Think First

Don't jump wholeheartedly into the first possible solution; think about what you're doing. Sit back and *think* about the problem you want to solve. Thinking costs nothing yet can save mondo amounts of time, effort, and psychological wear and tear. Think first before you issue that FORMAT command, before you copy that file, before you turn off your machine. Being in too much of a hurry now can cost you hours of grief later.

Write It Down

Witch Doctors are part of another realm, thus error messages that look like gibberish to us might be useful to them (of course, it might be gibberish to them too, but they just don't want to tell us). Being rescued doesn't mean you couldn't have done it yourself. In fact, if you play your cards right, you *can* do it yourself next time. If you get yourself in a jam, write down the problem and how you got out of it. Then, whenever you get stuck, consult your list to see if you had the same problem before. If so, great. You can look at the steps you took last time and fix things yourself.

If not, that's okay, too. Just write down how you fix the problem this time so that next time you'll know what to do.

Be specific; don't approximate error messages. If it beeped, write down any patterns (long-short-short). If you tried solutions, write down what you did and in what order (the order is as important as what you did). Write down how you fixed it this time. Write down all the steps you went through when you created something. Write down how you answered queries. Write down what you didn't do. Very often these notes will save your neck later.

Don't Move

When you're troubleshooting, one thing often leads to another, which leads to another, and you keep digging further as you chase the elusive problem.

So many times you find a problem and think "Hey — this one'll be easy." Ultimately, you find that you've landed the Queen Mother of All Iceberg Problems. Somewhere along the way, it begins to exceed your ability; the problem begins to win. You'll raise your eyes from the morass of unplugged cables, strewn manuals, and scribbled notes. Your brain will desperately whisper, "I'm over my head. I think I'm in trouble."

Moments like this can be great learning experiences. They can also be the last moments of your computer's useful life on the planet. Knowing when to call for help is a most valuable skill in computer troubleshooting. It saves wear and tear on you, your computer, and your witch doctor.

Epilogue

Once you reach this point, frantically resist the urge to try "just one more thing." Witch doctors often perform miracles but (equally as often) are seriously impaired by the "last thing" their acolyte tried. If a problem is serious enough that you've given every bit of skill and daring you possess chasing it to the ground, it's also important enough to make you swallow any remaining pride and speak the words "Help me; help my computer."

Once you've given up, don't go back. If you get a brainstorm and you're *positive* this will solve the problem, write down your thoughts and sit on your hands. Discuss your idea with the witch doctor. Don't attempt the resolution again. You might be taking that last step which separates you from the digital disaster.

Don't Be Afraid

I heard someone say once that people just need to take responsibility where their computers are concerned. Keep a positive, nonintimidated attitude. Basically, be a proactive user. Take charge of your PC. Take ownership. Divide and conquer. . . .

Know more about it than it knows about you. They're not as smart as some people think, you know. So they can add up a bunch of six-digit numbers fast — big deal.

Your computer is dead weight without your intervention. Make the best of it.

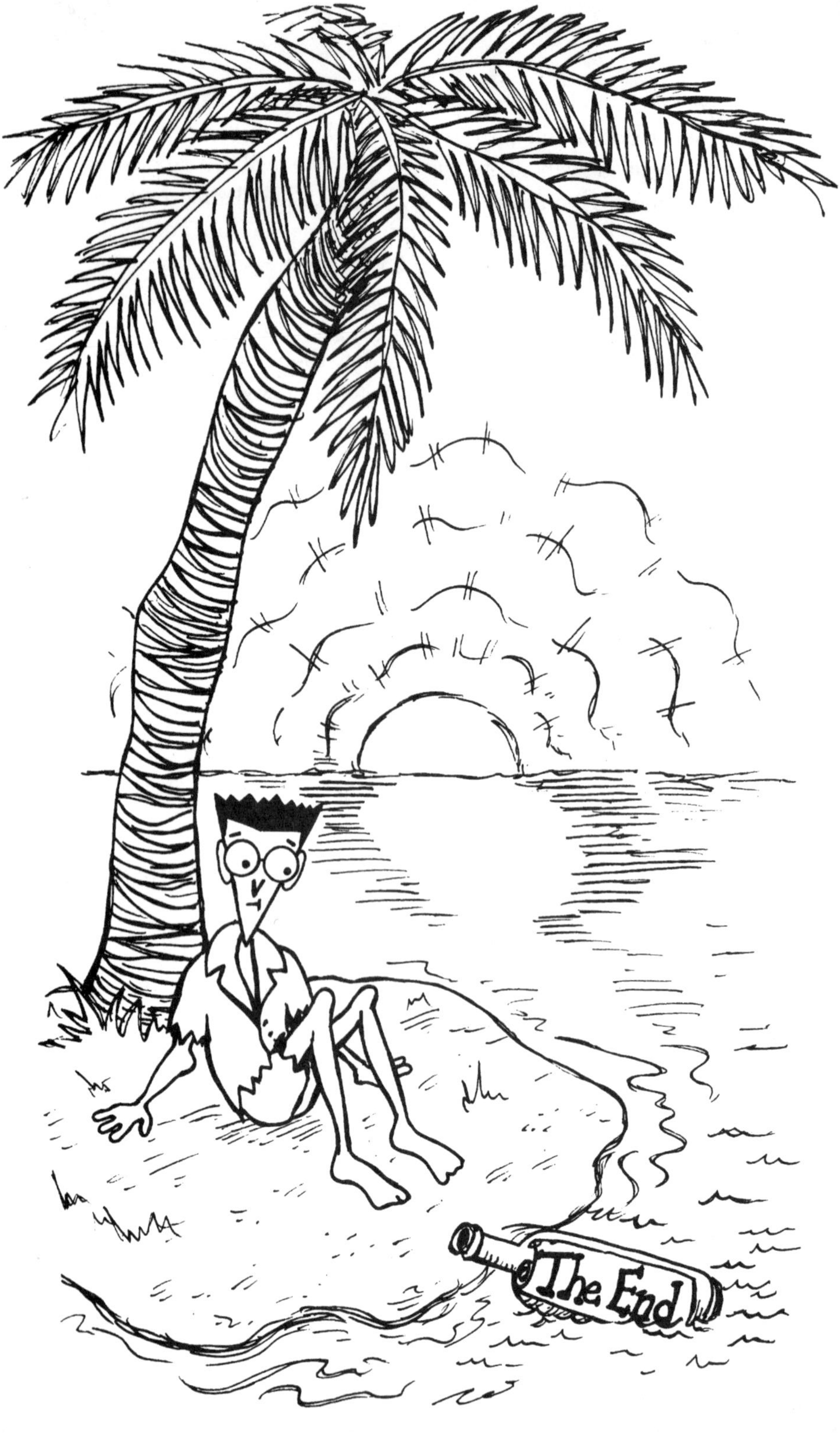
The End

Index

■ Symbols

386 Enhanced mode, 211-212
   DOS programs, 115-116, 118, 192, 196
   memory requirements, 31
   starting Windows, 32
   Windows won't start in, 202-203
386MAX memory manager, 35

■ A

Abnormal termination message, 214
About Program Manager command, 27, 94, 97, 115, 205
accidently formatting disks, 71-72, 87
active window, 58
AdLib, 185
Adobe Type Manager (ATM), 152
Alt key, 81
Always have a backup, 134, 221-222
AntiVirus, 98
APPEND (DOS) command, 29
Application still active message, 115, 132
application swap file. *See* swap file
APPS.INF file, 123
Are you sure you want to copy the selected files to message, 81
Are you sure you want to move the selected files to message, 81
Are you sure you want to remove the ... font? message, 157-158
associate, 77
Associate command, 77
ATM Control Panel, 152
ATM (Adobe Type Manager) fonts, 141, 152
   increasing font cache, 173
AUTOEXEC.BAT file, 28
   automatically changing, 223
   backing up, 19, 56
   bypassing, 20
   editing, 35-36
   extended memory programs, 214
   incompatible commands, 29
   information for witch doctor, 83
   LOADHIGH command, 211
   loading TSRs, 24
   modifications, 25
   PATH statement, 26, 36, 183
   printout, 93
   SET TEMP= statement, 166-167, 178
   SMARTDRV.EXE file, 94, 96, 189-190, 205
   TEMP= statement, 176
   avoiding bad advice, 169

■ B

backgrounds. *See* wallpaper
BACKUP (DOS) command, 82
backups, 80, 82, 221-222
   most recent, 93
   system configuration, 92
Bad command or file name message, 30
Bad or missing C:\WINDOWS\HIMEM.SYS message, 205
BAT file extension, 75
BMP file extension, 75
But it says multimedia, 197
By File Type command, 56, 75

■ C

Cancel (Ctrl-C) key combination, 223
Cannot find file (or one of its components). message, 77
Cannot format disk message, 86
Cannot print message, 178-179
Cannot rename FILENAME: Cannot find file message, 86
Cannot replace FILENAME: Access Denied message, 87
Cannot run program. Out of system resources. message, 62, 104
Cannot start application message, 104
Cascade command, 59
cascading windows, 59
CD-ROM
   can't read CD, 185-186
   CD seated, 185
   CD upside down, 185
   checking cables, 183
   checking installation, 183
   computer ignores, 182-183
   correct kind of disks, 185
   disk damaged, 185
   keeps spinning, 184-185
   problems, 73
   sound quality, 197-198
   Windows doesn't see, 183-184
CHKDSK (DOS) command, 33
CHKDSK /F (DOS) command, 20
clipboard
   can't paste from, 127-128
   clearing, 120
   DOS programs can't find, 116, 126-127
Clipboard Viewer, 118
color
   changing screen, 47
   printing problems, 180
Color icon, 47
commands
   About Program Manager, 27, 94, 97, 115, 205
   APPEND (DOS), 29
   Associate, 77
   BACKUP (DOS), 82
   By File Type, 56, 75
   Cascade, 59
   CHKDSK (DOS), 33
   CHKDSK /F (DOS), 20

Copy, 56, 78, 103
COPY (DOS), 42
DIR (DOS), 30, 172
Directory, 70
Edit, 118
Edit Copy, 118
Exit Windows, 115
EXPAND (DOS), 42, 205
FASTOPEN (DOS), 29
Fonts, 70, 119
FORMAT (DOS), 86
Format Disk, 22, 56
GRAPHICS (DOS), 29
incompatible, 29
Insert Object, 193
JOIN (DOS), 29
Links, 104
Mark, 118
MEM (DOS), 33, 94, 97, 207, 209
MSD (DOS), 209
New, 52
Paste Link, 103
Print, 162, 165-166
PRINT (DOS), 29
Properties, 87
Refresh, 73, 85
Rename, 86
Run, 49, 84-85, 95, 207
Search, 78, 87
Select Files, 80
sequence to start Windows, 30
SETUP /P, 49, 63
SHARE (DOS), 29
Tile, 59
Tree, 70
TREE (DOS), 30
UNDELETE (DOS), 84-85
Undo, 223
UNFORMAT (DOS), 72
WIN, 30
computer
  blank monitor, 16
  crashing sound and won't boot, 106
  dead, 14-15
  ignores CD-ROM, 182-183
  laptop battery down, 15
  locked up, 37-38, 147
  locks up during installation, 24-25
  plugged in, 15
  rebooting, 28
  sound, 186
  turned on, 15
  Windows starts when you turn it on, 35-36
computer stores and witch doctors, 57
computer user groups and witch doctors, 57
CONFIG.SYS file, 28
  automatically changing, 223
  backing up, 19, 56
  bypassing, 20
  DEVICE statements for RAMDrive and EMM386, 214

DEVICE= statement, 31
DEVICEHIGH= statement, 211
EMM386.EXE, 213
extended memory programs, 214
FILES= statement, 24-25, 29
HIMEM.SYS file, 120
HIMEM.SYS and EMM386.EXE before DEVICEHIGH command, 213
information for witch doctor, 83
loading HIMEM.SYS before DEVICE command, 213
modifications, 25
printout, 93
STACKS= statement, 38
Control menu, 118
  Alt+spacebar key combination, 60, 119
Control Panel, 27
  color, 47
  Fonts window, 137
  wallpaper, 47
conventional memory, not enough, 214
COPY (DOS) commands, 42
Copy command, 56, 78, 103
copying disks, unable to, 75-76
copying files vs. moving, 81
Could not print page 2 message, 179
Ctrl key, 81

D

data
  backing up before installation, 19
  DDE linking, 99
  garbled, 125-126
  linking, 99
  OLE linking, 99
  pasting, 99
  too many links, 102
data files, small, 201
DDE (dynamic data exchange), 101-103
  alarming messages, 101-102
  controlling updating, 104
  linking data, 99
  lost links, 103
  too many links, 102
  updating too often, 103-104
dead computer, 14-15
_default.pif file, 122
device drivers. *See* drivers
Device is being used by another application message, 196
Device menu, 193
DEVICE= statement, 31
DIR (DOS) command, 30, 172
directories
  collapsed display, 78
  correct, 30
  deleted, 78
  deleting without backup, 88

Index

display fonts, 70
DOS program in wrong, 124-125
missing, 63-64, 77-78
MSCDEX, 183
problems, 63-64
program icon won't work, 50
reinstalling Windows, 26
searching for, 78, 87
temp, 24, 176, 179
tree and file display problems, 70
WIN, 30
Directory command, 70
directory tree display problems, 70
disk cache, 205
disk compression programs, 21
disk drive
   is it okay, 72
   is disk in properly, 72
   unable to read disk format, 72
   wrong density disks, 86
Disk menu, 22, 56
disks
   accidently formatting, 71-72, 87
   bad spot, 80
   can someone else read it, 72
   enough room for programs, 95
   in drive properly, 72
   is it formatted, 72
   is it in drive, 72
   magnetized, 80
   old, 80
   unable to copy, 75-76
   unable to format, 86
   unable to see, 72
   Windows backup, 20
   wrong density in drive, 86
display
   awful, 39-40
   crowded, 71
   squat letters, 118-119
   WYSIWYG, 142
Divide by zero message, 104-105
DOC file extension, 75
documents
   changing old to TrueType font, 148, 150
   won't display in TrueType fonts, 154, 156
Don't be afraid, 36, 227
Don't make assumptions, 159, 223-224
Don't move, 226-227
Don't panic, 65, 225
DOS
   important files, 28
   pre-DOS 5.0 and accidently formatting disks, 87
   printing directly from, 167
   version required, 24
   version too old, 97
DOS 6
   AntiVirus, 98
   DoubleSpace, 21
   listing deleted files, 85
   MEMMAKER, 42, 197, 214
   Stacker, 21
DOS 6.2
   bypassing AUTOEXEC.BAT and CONFIG.SYS files, 20
   MSAV, 99
   ScanDisk, 20
   VSAFE, 99
DOS programs
   386 Enhanced mode, 115-116, 118, 192, 196
   application swap file, 121
   can't exit Windows, 115
   can't find clipboard, 116, 126-127
   can't get back to Windows, 127
   can't paste from clipboard, 127-128
   copying and pasting to Windows, 118
   crashing on network, 134
   forcing into windows, 116
   full screen, 115-116
   garbage when exiting, 119
   garbled data, 125-126
   graphics file problems, 128
   locking up, 131
   modifying PIF file, 116, 122-124
   new PIF file, 121-122
   no audio, 192
   not enough memory, 132-133
   odd display, 128, 130
   out of memory, 120-121
   PIF files, 115
   printer setup utility, 166
   printing from, 177-178
   running in background, 120-121
   squat letter display, 118-119
   Standard mode, 114, 116
   still running, 132
   TSR (terminate-and-stay-resident), 130-131
   turning Print Screen key back on, 177
   unable to run multiple, 121
   unable to use audio, 196
   won't run in Windows, 114
   wrong directory, 124-125
DoubleSpace, 21
downloading, 138
Dr. Watson, 64, 95, 98, 134
drag-and-drop feature
   adding programs to Startup group, 51
   moving and copying files, 81
drive E problems, 73
drivers, 24
   DEVICEHIGH= command, 213
   incompatible, 29
   loading, 212-213
   MSCDEX, 183
   mouse, 24
   printer, 24
   upper memory, 213
   video, 24
DRWATSON.LOG file, 64

E

Edit command, 118
Edit Copy command, 118
Edit menu, 103-104
embedded objects and error messages, 101-102
EMM386.EXE memory manager, 35, 202, 211
Error 20 message, 167, 170
Error in CONFIG.SYS, line 8 message, 40
error messages
  Abnormal termination, 214
  Application still active, 115, 132
  Are you sure you want to copy the selected files to, 81
  Are you sure you want to move the selected files to, 81
  Are you sure you want to remove the ... font?, 157-158
  Bad command or file name, 30
  Bad or missing C:\WINDOWS\HIMEM.SYS, 205
  Cannot find file (or one of its components)., 77
  Cannot format disk, 86
  Cannot print, 178, 179
  Cannot rename FILENAME: Cannot find file, 86
  Cannot replace FILENAME: Access Denied, 87
  Cannot run program. Out of system resources., 62, 104
  Cannot start application, 104
  copies of, 93
  Could not print page 2, 179
  DDE, 101-102
  Device is being used by another application, 196
  Divide by zero, 104-105
  Error 20, 167, 170
  Error in CONFIG.SYS, line 8, 40
  Error selecting drive. There is no disk in drive E, 197
  Extremely low on memory. Close applications and try again., 62-63
  File Manager, 86-87
  fonts, 146-147
  General printer error, 179
  General Protection Fault, 146
  Group file is damaged, 63
  Incorrect password; Check your screen save password and try again, 63
  Insufficient conventional memory, 214
  Insufficient memory to run the application, 132-133
  Internal stack overflow, 40-41
  Keyboard error, press F2 to continue, 41
  multimedia, 196-197
  No association exists, 77
  No fonts found, 158
  No matching files were found, 87
  Not enough memory, 105
  Not enough memory to load, 133
  Out of memory, 32, 41, 61, 198, 201
  PCL PRINTING WARNING: SOFT FONT PAGE LIMIT: Some fonts will be substituted, 170
  Permanent swap file corrupted, 133
  PCL Printing Warning: Soft font page limit, 158
  POST ERROR code 1102, 41-42
  Printer: Default Printer (QMS-PS 810 on LPT1:), 162
  Program groups are missing, 63
  System error, 134
  The application will not be able to use audio, 196
  The path D:\WINWORD\WINWORD.EXE is invalid, 63
  The printer on LPT1 is offline or not selected, 179
  The screen saver you are using is password protected., 48
  The working directory is invalid, 50, 63-64
  This application has violated system integrity, 134
  Unable to start Enhanced mode, 215
  witch doctors, 129
  You must have WINA20.386 in the root directory of the drive you booted from, 42
  Your program cannot be swapped out, 133
Error selecting drive. There is no disk in drive E message, 197
Escape key, 223
EXE file extension, 75
Exit Windows command, 115
EXPAND (DOS) command, 42, 205
experienced coworkers, 57
extended memory, not enough, 214
Extremely low on memory. Close applications and try again. message, 62-63

F

FASTOPEN (DOS) command, 29
file extensions, linking with program, 77
File Manager, 56, 63
  customizing file display, 75
  doesn't see disk, 72
  erroneous file display, 73
  error messages, 86-87
  missing graphics files, 74-75
  problems, 67-85
  unreadable screen, 70
File menu, 49, 52, 56, 77-78, 80, 84, 86-87, 95, 115, 162, 165-166, 193
files
  APPS.INF, 123

Index

AUTOEXEC.BAT, 28
backup, 80, 82, 84
checking for viruses, 99
closing up unnecessary, 201
CONFIG.SYS, 28
contiguous selection, 79
copying to disk, 87
corrupted, 26, 33, 63
_default.pif, 122
deleting necessary, 84-85
deselecting, 80
display fonts, 70
dragging, 81
DRWATSON.LOG, 64
embedding objects, 101-102
erroneous display, 73
FINSTALL.DIR, 152
forever selected, 79-80
garbled data, 125-126
graphics files missing, 74-75
HIMEM.SYS, 31
INFO.MSD, 92
inserting sound, 193-194
interference when saving, 80
missing, 26, 33
MORICONS.DLL, 51
moving off hard disk and losing floppy, 87-88
moving vs. copying, 81
no associated application, 76-77
noncontiguous selection, 79
OLECLI.DLL, 100
OLESVR.DLL, 100
PROGMAN.EXE, 51
properties, 87
scrambled, 80
searching for, 78, 87
SETUP.TXT, 211
SMARTDRV.EXE, 205
SYSTEM.INI, 31
TESTPS.TXT, 171
unable to rename, 86
unable to select, 78-79
undeleting, 84-85
WIN.INI, 31
write-protected, 87
FILES= statement, 24-25, 29
FINSTALL.DIR file, 152
floppy disk, copying files from hard disk and losing, 87-88
Font command, 119
Font dialog box, 119
Font Installer, 136, 138, 140
 renaming fonts, 157
 unable to locate, 139
fonts
 accidently deleting, 159
 adding to system, 138-139
 ATM, 141, 152
 available on printer, 140
 bad or invisible, 154, 156
 can print other, 140
 changing document to TrueType, 148, 150
 correct selected, 172
 corrupted, 146-147
 different on-screen than printed, 141-143
 downloadable missing after Windows reinstallation, 156
 downloading, 138
 enough printer memory, 141
 error messages, 146-147
 installed correctly, 140-141
 installing, 138-139
 jaggies, 141
 large characters are blotchy, 141
 leaving in network directory, 154
 missing but showing up in program, 144
 mixing TrueType with other fonts, 145-146
 MS Sans Serif, 159
 no-name, 137
 non-TrueType, 139
 nonprinting soft fonts, 136-137
 printer, 143
 problems, 146-150, 159
 programs can't find deleted, 159
 raster, 138, 143
 renaming, 157
 running out of hard disk space, 153-154
 scalable, 138
 screen, 143
 Small Font, 137
 soft, 138
 summary file, 152
 tiny sizes, 137
 too many, 147, 175
 TrueType, 137-138, 141-146
 two with same name, 157
 unable to find files, 158
 using fewer, 150, 173
 vector, 138
 verifying removal, 157-158
 won't print, 139-141
Fonts command, 70
FORMAT (DOS) command, 86
Format Disk command, 22, 56

■ G

General printer error message, 179
General Protection Fault message, 146
General Protection Faults (GPFs), 95
 DOS programs, 134
 recording, 64
 Windows programs, 96-98
Generic/Text Only printer driver, 162
Generic/Text printer driver, 26
GIF file extension, 75
Go back to the last fork in the road, 84
Go back to the very beginning, 79

Go to another tree, 76
GRAPHICS (DOS) command, 29
graphics card
  installing correct, 46
  multimedia software doesn't work, 194-195
graphics driver, wrong one installed, 40
graphics file
  missing, 74-75
  problems, 128
  too big to print, 175
Group file is damaged message, 63
Group Window (Alt+Esc) key combination, 59, 114
GRP file extension, 56

H

hard disk
  backing up data, 19
  deleting unnecessary programs, 20-21
  low on storage space, 133
  making room for Windows, 20-21
  not enough room, 176, 179
  running out of font room, 153-154
  swap file room, 150
  verifying before installing Windows, 20
hardware
  manuals, 93
  setup and Windows, 98
  wrong installation, 33
Help menu, 27, 94, 97, 205
Hewlett-Packard printer
  error message, 167, 170
  maximum downloadable soft fonts, 170
  maximum number of fonts used, 158
hidden windows, displaying, 59
HIMEM.SYS file, 31, 120, 202, 211
HPPCL soft fonts, installing, 139

I

icons
  can't remember names, 65
  changing, 51
  Color, 47
  problems, 50-51
  Program Manager, 45
  Setup, 33
  Tile, 47
incompatible commands and drivers, 29
Incorrect password; Check your screen save password and try again message, 63
INFO.MSD file, 92
INI file extension, 56
Insert Object command, 193
installation
  computer locks up, 24-25
  is Windows installed, 30

slow, 21
wrong graphics driver, 40
Insufficient conventional memory message, 214
Insufficient memory to run the application message, 132-133
Internal stack overflow message, 40-41
interrupts (IRQs), 40-41, 188
  mouse, 38
  sound board problems, 188
Isolate the problem, 180, 220-221

J

jaggies, 141
JOIN (DOS) command, 29

K

key combinations
  Alt+Enter (Window), 116, 118
  Alt+Esc (Group Window), 59, 114
  Alt+spacebar (Control menu), 60, 119
  Alt+Tab (Program Window), 59, 132
  Ctrl+Alt+Del (Warm Boot), 28, 94
  Ctrl+Esc (Task List), 58, 59, 115
  Ctrl-Break (Stop), 223
  Ctrl-C (Cancel), 223
keyboard
  nothing happens, 39
  plugged in, 39
  spills on, 39
  unplugged, 41
  works with DOS, 39
Keyboard error, press F2 to continue message, 41
keys
  Alt, 81
  Ctrl, 81
  Escape, 223
  Print Screen, 116, 176-177
Know how to undo things, 198, 222-223

L

laptop battery charged, 15
linking data, 99
Links command, 104

M

Main group, 27
Mark command, 118
Media Player
  setting, 193
  won't play, 192-193
MEM (DOS) command, 33, 94, 97, 207, 209
MEMMAKER, 33-34, 42, 120, 189, 197, 201, 214
memory
  386 Enhanced mode, 31

Index

adding, 201-202
conflict between Windows and sound board, 189
DOS programs out of memory, 120-121
enough, 26, 203
enough to run Windows, 31
management, 199-215
multimedia requirements, 198
no room for TSR (terminate-and-stay-resident) programs, 211
not enough, 33, 35, 41-42, 132-133
not enough extended, 214
optimized, 34, 189, 201
out of memory, 200-202
printers, 141, 173
printing, 178-179
programs not releasing, 61
requirements, 20-21, 31, 203
Standard mode, 31
too many fonts, 147
TrueType fonts, 150
which portion system is using, 207, 209
memory managers, 202
  386MAX, 35
  EMM386.EXE, 35
messages. *See* error messages
microprocessor and video clips, 195
modes, 27
running in right, 35
which to start Windows in, 32
monitors
awful display, 39-40
blank, 16
checking for power light, 16
connecting to another system, 16
dead, 15
plugged in, 16
turning on/off, 16
unconventional video driver, 25
wrong display entered, 33
MORICONS.DLL file, 51
mouse
conflicts, 37
dead, 37
interrupts, 38
locks up computer, 37-38
non-Microsoft, 37
plugged in, 38
stuck, 37-38
stuck pointer, 38-39
works in other applications, 37
works with DOS programs, 39
mouse drivers, 24
installed, 39
MOUSE.COM, 39
MOUSE.SYS, 39
not loaded, 37
MOUSE.COM driver, 39
MOUSE.INI file, backing up, 56
MOUSE.SYS driver, 39
moving files vs. copying, 81
MS Sans Serif font, accidentally deleting, 159
MSAV, 99
MSCDEX directory, 183
MSCDEX driver, 183
MSD, 92, 123
printout, 93
MSD (DOS) command, 209
multimedia
can't read CD, 185-186
CD-ROM keeps spinning, 184-185
computer ignores CD-ROM, 182-183
error messages, 196-197
getting sound out, 186
inserting sound in file, 193-194
Media Player won't play, 192-193
memory requirements, 198
no audio in DOS programs, 192
old software and hardware won't run, 197
Out of memory errors, 198
problems, 197-198
software doesn't work with graphics card, 194-195
sound board keeps repeating sound, 188-189
sound board silent, 187-188
sound locks Windows, 190
Sound Recorder, 193
unsupported sound driver, 190
video clips move in slow motion, 195-196
Windows doesn't see CD-ROM, 183-184
Multimedia Extensions, 184
installed, 187-188

N

networks, 83
DOS programs crashing, 134
everyone down, 15
group windows problems, 54
leaving fonts in directory, 154
New command, 52
No association exists message, 77
No fonts found message, 158
No matching files were found message, 87
no-name font, 137
non-Microsoft mouse, 37
non-TrueType fonts, 139
Norton Disk Doctor, 20
Not enough memory message, 105
Not enough memory to load message, 133
Notepad, editing AUTOEXEC.BAT file, 35

O

OLE (object linking and embedding), 100-101
linking data, 99
problems, 100
OLECLI.DLL file, 100
OLESVR.DLL file, 100

on-line forums and witch doctors, 57
on-line services and viruses, 99
on-screen pointer, locks up, 33
operating system information, 83
Options menu, 70
Out of memory message, 32, 41, 61, 198, 201

P

Paste Link command, 103
PATH statement, 26, 30, 36
paths, 63
PCL printer
   problems, 170-171
   soft fonts, 171
PCL PRINTING WARNING: SOFT FONT PAGE LIMIT: Some fonts will be substituted message, 170
peripherals, special, 83
permanent swap file. *See* swap file
Permanent swap file corrupted message, 133
PIF Editor, 119, 124
PIF (Program Information File) file, 119
   can't find clipboard, 127
   can't get back to Windows, 127
   can't paste from clipboard, 128
   editing, 119
   garbled data, 126
   graphics file problems, 128
   modifying, 116
   new, 121-122
   odd display, 128, 130
   should you modify, 122-124
   Startup Directory: statement, 124
   TSR (terminate-and-stay-resident) programs, 130-131
PIF file extension, 124
PLC Printing Warning: Soft font page limit message, 158
ports
   competition for printer, 178
   something else plugged in, 166
   verifying selection, 177
POST (Power-On Self-Test) errors, 41-42
POST ERROR code 1102 message, 41-42
PostScript, character size limitations, 171
PostScript printer driver, 162
PostScript printers
   checking settings, 175
   error codes, 175
   flashing lights but no printing, 174-175
   loose cable, 175
   lower resolution printing, 175
   out of memory, 171
   printing half page only, 173
   selecting wrong printer, 175
   TrueType fonts, 156
PRINT (DOS) command, 29
Print command, 162
   grayed, 165-166

Print Screen key, 116
   won't work, 176-177
Print Setup dialog box, 165
   selecting printer, 175
printer drivers, 24, 168
   correct, 166
   current, 172
   Generic/Text, 26, 162
   getting correct, 163
   installing, 162
   listing name, 168
   PostScript, 162
   similar models, 26
   unknown, 25-26
   updating, 168
   version, 168
printer fonts, 143
Printer: Default Printer (QMS-PS 810 on LPT1:) message, 162
printers
   adding memory, 173
   cables okay, 165
   cables tight, 165
   can print other fonts, 140
   cartridge okay, 140
   checking options, 173
   checking settings, 177-178
   correct driver, 166
   correct installed, 172
   current driver, 172
   don't see non-TrueType fonts, 139-141
   enough memory, 141
   fonts available, 140
   freezing Windows, 175-176
   hardware dead, 164-166
   hardware problems, 179
   lower resolution, 179
   maximum number of fonts used, 158
   not enough memory, 173
   not on install list, 162-163
   out of RAM, 171
   paper jam, 165
   paper loaded, 165
   PCL, 170
   plugged in, 165
   PostScript, 171
   PostScript and TrueType fonts, 156
   printing from other programs, 172
   printing TrueType fonts, 144
   ready light on, 165
   selecting similar type, 162
   selection, 139, 165
   self-test, 172
   setting default, 164
   setting up in Windows, 166
   setup utility, 166
   sharing, 165
   soft fonts, 136-137
   software dead, 166-167
   something else plugged in port, 166

Index

tightening cables, 172
turned on, 165
unable to select, 162
unknown driver, 25-26
wrong one always chosen, 163-164
wrong one selected, 162
Printers dialog box, 139, 179
printing
  color, 180
  directly from DOS, 167
  graphics file too big, 175
  half page only, 173
  lower resolution, 173
  not enough memory, 178-180
  Print Screen won't work, 176-177
  problems, 180
  screen, 172
  too many fonts, 175
  unable to, 165-166
  very slow, 178
  weird characters, 172
problems
  accidently deleting WIN.INI file, 42
  accidently formatting necessary disk, 87
  always have a backup, 221-222
  blank monitor, 16
  CD-ROM, 73
  color printing, 180
  computer crashing sound and won't boot, 106
  computer doesn't work, 14-15
  copying and pasting from DOS programs, 118
  crowded display, 71
  deleting directory without backup, 88
  deleting needed files, 84-85
  directories, 63-64
  disappearing program groups, 49
  don't be afraid, 227
  don't make assumptions, 223-224
  don't move, 226-227
  drive E, 73
  file has no associated application, 76-77
  File Manager, 67-85
  fonts, 146-150, 159
  general protection faults (GPFs), 134
  hanging up Windows, 106
  icons, 50-51
  installing program in different groups, 65
  isolating, 220-221
  know how to undo things, 222-223
  large characters are blotchy, 141
  missing directories, 77-78
  moving files off hard disk and losing floppy, 87-88
  multimedia, 197-198
  network group windows, 54
  not enough memory, 42
  not enough RAM (random access memory), 62-63
  OLE (object linking and embedding), 100
  panic, 225

PCL printer, 170-171
PostScript printer flashes but does not print, 174-175
printing, 180
printing half page only, 173
PROGMAN.INI file keeps running, 64-65
Program Manager, 43-65
raster fonts, 143
scrambled files, 80
screen saver will not go away, 48
Setup, 24-25
squat letters on display, 118-119
start over and try again, 221
startup, 14-42
swap file, 209-210
think first, 225-226
too many fonts, 147
unable to copy disks, 75-76
unable to select file, 78-79
Windows program installation program quit, 90-91
windows, 55, 58-60
write it down, 226
PROGMAN.EXE file, 51
PROGMAN.INI file, keeps running, 64-65
program disks, 93
program groups
  adding program item, 52-53
  disappearing, 49
  installing program in different, 65
  missing programs, 52-53
  problems, 63
  rebuilding default, 49
Program groups are missing message, 63
program item, 49
  adding to program group, 52-53
  can't remember names and icon names, 65
Program Item dialog box, Working Directory: line, 125
Program Item Properties dialog box, 51
  finding programs, 50
Program Manager, 27
  disappearing program groups, 49
  distorted display, 46
  doesn't look the same as everyone else's, 53-54
  icon, 45
  problems, 43-65
  staying open, 45-46
Program Window (Alt+Tab) key combination, 59, 132
programs
  accepting from people you know, 99
  accidently deleted, 50
  Adobe Type Manager (ATM), 152
  AntiVirus, 98
  any other running, 30
  can't find deleted fonts, 159
  closing unnecessary, 120, 201
  correct font selected, 172

deleting unnecessary, 20-21
disk compression, 21
DOS, 111-134
Dr. Watson, 64, 95, 98, 134
EMM386.EXE, 202
fonts missing but showing up, 144
HIMEM.SYS, 120, 202
icon won't work, 50
installing in different groups, 65
launching by clicking data file, 76-77
linking with file extension, 77
MEMMAKER, 33, 120
missing, 63
missing from program group, 52-53
moved, 50
MSAV, 99
MSD, 92, 123
Norton Disk Doctor, 20
not associated with file, 76-77
not installing options, 201
not releasing memory, 61
OLE support, 100
printing from other, 172
putting in Startup group, 36
Quick Unerase, 85
SmartDrive, 96, 205
starting up, 51
Swapdisk, 202
switching between DOS and Windows, 114
UNDELETE, 85
UnFormat, 71-72, 87
Virtual Memory Manager (VMM), 202
VSAFE, 99
Windows, 89-98
what you are using, 83
windows lost, 58-59
Windows Uninstall, 90-91
Properties command, 87

Q

Quick Unerase, 85

R

RAM (random-access memory), 16
  device not loaded, 196
  efficiently using, 202
  making most of, 120
  not enough, 62-63, 97, 105, 133, 176
  printer out of, 171
  problems, 94
  video clips, 195-196
raster fonts, 138, 143
  problems, 143
  screen and printer fonts, 143
real mode, 206
Refresh command, 73, 85
reinstallation problems, 26

Rename command, 86
road signs, 6
  But it says multimedia, 197
  Font magic, 154
  Go back to the very beginning, 79
  Go to another tree, 76
  important DOS files, 28
  You know you need more memory when..., 213
Run command, 49, 84-85, 95, 207
Run dialog box, 98

S

satchels, 5
  file backups, 82
  printer drivers, 168
  system configuration backup, 92
  Windows System Disk, 22
scalable fonts, 138
ScanDisk, 20
screen
  changing color, 47
  fonts different on-screen, 141-143
  fonts unreadable, 70
  long time to update, 150, 153-154
  printing, 172
  unable to print, 176-177
  windows almost off, 59-60
screen fonts, 143
screen savers, 47-48
  passwords, 63
  Starfield Simulation, 48
  will not go away, 48
scrolls, 6
  Always have a backup, 134, 221-222
  Call the Witch Doctor, 220
  Don't be afraid, 36, 227
  Don't make assumptions, 159, 223-224
  Don't move, 242, 226-227
  Don't panic, 65, 225
  Isolate the problem, 180, 220-221
  Know how to undo things, 198, 222-223
  Start over and try again, 206, 221
  Think first, 88, 225-226
  Write it down, 106, 226
Search command, 78, 87
Select Files command, 80
Setup program
  incompatible commands, 29
  installing correct graphics card, 46
  installing correct graphics driver, 40
  monitor type, 25
  new PIF files, 122
  problems, 24-25
  TSR programs and, 28
  unknown printer driver, 25-26
SETUP /P command, 49, 63
Setup icon, 33

Index

SETUP.INF file, incompatible drivers, 29
SETUP.TXT file, 211
SHARE (DOS) command, 29
SHELL= statement, 54
shells, 54
sign posts
   DOS programs and PIF files, 115
   Go back to the last fork in the road, 84
slow installation, 21
Small Font, 137
SmartDrive, 96, 205
SMARTDRV.EXE file, 205
   in AUTOEXEC.BAT file, 94
smoke signals, 6
   Abnormal termination, 214
   Application still active, 132
   Are you sure you want to remove the ... font?, 157-158
   Cannot format disk, 86
   Cannot print, 178-179
   Cannot rename FILENAME: Cannot find file, 86
   Cannot replace FILENAME: Access Denied, 87
   Cannot run program. Out of system resources., 62, 104
   Cannot start application, 104
   Could not print page 2, 179
   Device is being used by another application, 196
   Divide by zero, 104-105
   Error selecting drive. There is no disk in drive E, 197
   Extremely low on memory. Close applications and try again., 62-63
   General printer error, 179
   Group file is damaged, 63
   Incorrect password; Check your screen save password and try again, 63
   Insufficient conventional memory, 214
   Insufficient memory to run the application, 132-133
   No fonts found, 158
   No matching files were found, 87
   Not enough memory, 105
   Not enough memory to load, 133
   Permanent swap file corrupted, 133
   PLC Printing Warning: Soft font page limit, 158
   Program groups are missing, 63
   The application will not be able to use audio, 196
   The path D:\WINWORD\WINWORD.EXE is invalid, 63
   The printer on LPT1 is offline or not selected, 179
   The working directory is invalid, 63-64
   Unable to start Enhanced mode, 215
   Your program cannot be swapped out, 133
soft fonts, 138
   adding or deleting, 152

HPPCL, 139
   maximum downloadable, 170
   nonprinting, 136-137
   PCL printer, 171
   printers, 136-137
   reinstalling Windows and, 156
software manuals, 93
sound boards, 185
   AdLib, 185
   correctly installed, 187
   fries Windows, 197
   installation software, 187
   IRQ problems, 188
   keep repeating sound, 188-189
   locks Windows, 190
   memory conflict with Windows, 189
   silent, 187-188
   sound driver selected, 188
   SoundBlaster, 185
   unsupported sound driver, 190
sound drivers
   correct selected, 193
   selected, 188
   unsupported, 190
sound files, 193
Sound Recorder, 184, 193
SoundBlaster, 185
sounds
   getting out of computer, 186
   inserting in file, 193-194
   recording, 184
stack, 38, 40-41
Stacker, 21
STACKS= statement, 38
standalone machine, 83
Standard mode, 203, 211-212
   DOS programs, 114, 116
   forcing Windows to start in, 31-33
   memory requirements, 31
   unable to start Windows, 215
Starfield Simulation, 48
Start over and try again, 206, 221
startup problems, 14-42
Startup group, adding programs, 51
stepping stones, 5
   can print other fonts, 140
   can someone else read disk, 72
   changing text fonts, 139-140
   clearing clipboard, 120
   closing unnecessary programs, 120
   closing wallpaper, 120
   correctly installed sound board, 187
   disk in drive properly, 72
   DOS programs running in background, 120-121
   enough memory, 31, 203
   enough printer memory, 141
   Error in CONFIG.SYS, line 8, 40
   font available on printer, 140
   font installed correctly, 140-141

forcing Windows to start, 203
full-screen windows, 120
HIMEM.SYS, 31, 120
Internal stack overflow, 40-41
is disk formatted, 72
is disk in drive, 72
Keyboard error, press F2 to continue, 41
MEMMAKER and HIMEM.SYS, 120
minimizing open windows, 120
Multimedia Extensions installed, 187-188
Out of memory, 41
plugged in printers, 165
POST ERROR code 1102, 41-42
printer cables okay, 165
printer cables tight, 165
printer cartridge okay, 140
printer paper jam, 165
printer paper loaded, 165
printer ready light on, 165
printers turned on, 165
RAM (random access memory) problems, 94
sharing printers, 165
SMARTDRV.EXE in AUTOEXEC.BAT file, 94
sound board installation software, 187
sound driver selected, 188
SYSTEM.INI file, 31
total computer lockup, 94
TSRs unloaded, 31
unable to read disk format, 72
Windows program installation disks inserted properly, 94
WIN.INI file, 31
wrong version of Windows, 203, 205
You must have WINA20.386 in the root directory of the drive you booted from message, 42
Stop (Ctrl-Break) key combination, 223
Survival Disk, 19, 56
swap files, 121
  controlling, 202
  corrupted, 133
  problems, 209-210
  rebuilding, 133
  room on hard disks, 150
  temporary or permanent, 209-210
Swapdisk, 202
system
  adding fonts, 138-139
  configuration backup, 92
  information about components, 123
  too many fonts, 147
  type information, 83
  which portion of memory using, 207, 209
System Disk, 22
System error message, 134
SYSTEM.INI file, 31
  backing up, 54, 56
  SHELL= statement, 54

T

Task List (Ctrl+Esc) key combination, 58-59, 115
techie terms, 5
  associate, 77
  DDE (dynamic data exchange), 103
  disk cache, 205
  downloading, 138
  driver, 24
  General Protection Faults (GPFs), 98
  IRQ, 188
  memory manager, 202
  mouse driver, 24
  OLE (object linking and embedding), 100
  PIF (Program Information File), 119
  printer driver, 24
  program item, 49
  RAM (random-access memory), 16
  raster fonts, 138
  scalable fonts, 138
  soft fonts, 138
  sound boards, 185
  TSR (terminate-and-stay-resident) programs, 20
  vector fonts, 138
  video clips, 193
  video driver, 24
technical support staff, 57
TEMP directory, 24, 176, 179
TESTPS.TXT file, 171
text, changing fonts, 139-141
The application will not be able to use audio message, 196
The path D:\WINWORD\WINWORD.EXE is invalid message, 63
The printer on LPT1 is offline or not selected message, 179
The screen saver you are using is password protected. message, 48
The working directory is invalid message, 50, 63-64
Think first, 88, 225-226
This application has violated system integrity message, 134
Tile command, 59
Tile icon, 47
tiling windows, 59
Tools menu, 82, 98
trainers at computer training centers, 57
TREE (DOS) command, 30
Tree command, 70
TrueType fonts, 141-143
  changing old documents, 148, 150
  do I have, 137-138
  installing, 138
  memory, 150
  mixing with other fonts, 145-146
  PostScript printers, 156
  printing, 144

Index

video drivers, 156
won't display document, 154, 156
TSR (terminate-and-stay-resident) programs, 20, 24, 97
   causing problems, 27-28
   loading in upper memory, 211
   no room for, 211
   PIF files, 130-131
   removing, 28
   shutting off, 201
   unloaded, 31, 35
typing errors, starting up Windows, 30

U

Unable to start Enhanced mode message, 215
UNDELETE (DOS) command, 84-85
UNDELETE program, 85
Undo command, 223
UnFormat, 87
UNFORMAT (DOS) command, 72
UnFormat program, 71-72
Unrecoverable Application Error (UAE) and Windows programs, 96

V

vector fonts, 138
video clips, 193
   adjusting speed, 196
   microprocessor and, 195
   move in slow motion, 195-196
   RAM (random access memory), 195-196
video driver, 24
   TrueType fonts, 156
   unconventional, 25
View menu, 56, 70, 75
Virtual Memory Manager (VMM), 202
viruses
   accepting programs, 99
   checking files, 99
   crashing computer, 106
   downloading programs, 99
   protection, 98-99
   Windows programs, 98-99
VSAFE, 99

W

wallpaper
   changing, 46-47
   closing, 120
Warm Boot (Ctrl+Alt+Del) key combination, 28, 94
WAV file extension, 193
WAV files, 193
weird characters, printing, 172
WIN command, 30
WIN directory, 30
WIN.INI file, 31
   accidently deleting, 42
   backing up, 54, 56
WINA20.386 file in wrong place, 42
Window (Alt+Enter) key combination, 116, 118
Window menu, 59, 73, 85
windows
   active, 58
   almost off-screen, 59-60
   cascading, 59
   closing, 41
   displaying hidden, 59
   dragging, 60
   forcing DOS programs into, 116
   full-screen, 120
   large on-screen, 55
   lost program, 58-59
   maximizing, 55
   minimizing open, 120
   problems, 55, 58-60
   resizing border thickness, 58
   skinny borders, 55, 58
   tiling, 59
   too many open, 71
   trouble arranging, 59
Windows
   backup disks, 20
   basic necessities, 17
   before installing, 17, 19-20
   can't get back from DOS, 127
   character size limitations, 171
   conflict with programs, 95
   corrupted files, 26
   difference between modes, 211-212
   doesn't see CD-ROM, 183-184
   downloadable fonts are missing after reinstallation, 156
   forcing start, 203
   forcing start in Standard mode, 31-33
   graphics file problems, 128
   hanging up, 106
   hardware setup, 98
   is it installed, 30
   memory conflict with sound board, 189
   memory requirements, 20-21
   missing files, 26
   modes, 27
   new PIF files, 122
   printer freezing, 175-176
   real mode, 206
   restarting, 201
   running slow, 34-35
   setting up printer, 166
   sound board fries, 197
   sound locks, 190
   Standard mode, 203
   starts and hangs, 32-34
   starts up every time computer starts up, 35-36

System Disk, 22
too much going on, 104
unable to find, 30
unable to start in Standard mode, 215
verifying hard disk, 20
what mode to start in, 32, 205
will not start, 30-32
won't let you exit, 115
won't start in 386 Enhanced mode, 202-203
wrong version, 203, 205
Windows programs, 89-98
　cannot print from, 177-178
　conflict with Windows, 95
　corrupted files, 106
　dividing by zero, 104-105
　enough disk storage, 95
　General Protection Faults (GPFs), 96-98
　hanging up Windows, 106
　installation disks inserted properly, 94
　installation program quit, 90-91
　insufficient memory to continue, 214
　linking data, 99
　loading into high memory, 98
　multiple lockups, 95
　not supporting DDE, 103
　prior problems, 98
　right filename and path, 104
　stalled, 94-95
　total lockup, 94
　uninstalling, 90-91
　Unrecoverable Application Error (UAE), 96
　viruses, 98-99
Windows Uninstall, 90, 91
Windows Write, editing AUTOEXEC.BAT file, 35
witch doctors, 5
　abuse, 191
　asking for clarification, 155
　AUTOEXEC.BAT and CONFIG.SYS file information, 83
　avoiding bad advice, 169
　being kind, 191
　computer stores, 57
　computer user groups, 57
　copies of error messages, 93
　describing problems, 155
　environmental changes, 129
　error messages, 129
　experienced coworkers, 57
　getting second opinions, 169
　hardware and software manuals, 93
　having information ready for, 83
　how often problem occurs, 129
　interacting with, 155
　listening carefully, 155
　most recent backup, 93
　MSD printout, 93
　networks or standalone machine, 83
　new hardware/software, 129
　on-line forums, 57
　operating system information, 83
　printouts of CONFIG.SYS and AUTOEXEC.BAT files, 93
　program disks, 93
　programs used, 83
　special peripherals, 83
　staying out of the way, 155
　taking notes, 155
　technical support staff, 57
　thanking, 155
　trainers at computer training centers, 57
　type of system information, 83
　what died, 129
　what happened last, 129
　what stuff to have ready for, 93
　what to tell about problem, 129
　what you've tried, 129
　when it last worked, 129
　when to call, 220
　where to find, 57
　who they are, 23
　Yellow Pages, 57
words of wisdom, 6
　Adobe Type Manager (ATM), 152
　Control Panel, 27
　Dr. Watson, 64
　MEMMAKER, 34
　MSD, 123
　Program Manager, 27
　SmartDrive, 96
　Sound Recorder, 184
　TrueType fonts, 142
　Windows Survival Disk, 56
　Windows Uninstall, 91
Write it down, 106, 226
write-protected files, 87
WYSIWYG display, 142

Y

Yellow Pages and witch doctors, 57
You know you need more memory when..., 213
You must have WINA20.386 in the root directory of the drive you booted from message, 42
Your program cannot be swapped out message, 133

Z

zero, dividing by, 104-105

IDG BOOKS WORLDWIDE REGISTRATION CARD

RETURN THIS REGISTRATION CARD FOR FREE CATALOG

Title of this book: S.O.S. For Windows

My overall rating of this book: ❏ Very good [1] ❏ Good [2] ❏ Satisfactory [3] ❏ Fair [4] ❏ Poor [5]

How I first heard about this book:

❏ Found in bookstore; name: [6] _____   ❏ Book review: [7] _____
❏ Advertisement: [8] _____   ❏ Catalog: [9] _____
❏ Word of mouth; heard about book from friend, co-worker, etc.: [10]   ❏ Other: [11] _____

What I liked most about this book: _____

What I would change, add, delete, etc., in future editions of this book: _____

Other comments: _____

Number of computer books I purchase in a year: ❏ 1 [12] ❏ 2-5 [13] ❏ 6-10 [14] ❏ More than 10 [15]

I would characterize my computer skills as: ❏ Beginner [16] ❏ Intermediate [17] ❏ Advanced [18] ❏ Professional [19]

I use ❏ DOS [20] ❏ Windows [21] ❏ OS/2 [22] ❏ Unix [23] ❏ Macintosh [24] ❏ Other: [25] _____ (please specify)

I would be interested in new books on the following subjects:
(please check all that apply, and use the spaces provided to identify specific software)

❏ Word processing: [26]   ❏ Spreadsheets: [27]
❏ Data bases: [28]   ❏ Desktop publishing: [29]
❏ File Utilities: [30]   ❏ Money management: [31]
❏ Networking: [32]   ❏ Programming languages: [33]
❏ Other: [34]

I use a PC at (please check all that apply): ❏ home [35] ❏ work [36] ❏ school [37] ❏ other: [38] _____

The disks I prefer to use are ❏ 5.25 [39] ❏ 3.5 [40] ❏ other: [41] _____

I have a CD ROM: ❏ yes [42] ❏ no [43]

I plan to buy or upgrade computer hardware this year: ❏ yes [44] ❏ no [45]

I plan to buy or upgrade computer software this year: ❏ yes [46] ❏ no [47]

Name: _____   Business title: [48] _____
Type of Business: [49] _____
Address (❏ home [50] ❏ work [51]/Company name: _____
Street/Suite# _____
City [52]/State [53]/Zipcode [54]: _____   Country [55] _____

❏ **I liked this book!**
You may quote me by name in future IDG Books Worldwide promotional materials.

My daytime phone number is _____

IDG BOOKS
THE WORLD OF COMPUTER KNOWLEDGE

❏ **YES!**
Please keep me informed about IDG's World of Computer Knowledge. Send me the latest IDG Books catalog.

BUSINESS REPLY MAIL
FIRST CLASS MAIL   PERMIT NO. 2605   SAN MATEO, CALIFORNIA

IDG Books Worldwide
155 Bovet Road Suite 310
San Mateo CA 94402-9833

NO POSTAGE
NECESSARY
IF MAILED
IN THE
UNITED STATES